From
Letters
to
Leaders:

Redefining New Member
Education and Leveraging
Belonging to Eliminate Hazing

By

Michael Ayalon and the
Greek University Team

Contents

Introduction

Michael Ayalon

I hope that you have already read the first book in this series, *From Letters to Leaders: Creating Impact on Your College Campus and Beyond*. If not, pick it up today on Amazon! It covers a wide range of topics that are relevant on college campuses today, such as sexual assault prevention, alcohol/drug abuse prevention, hazing prevention, mental health, majority privilege, healthy masculinity, healthy relationships, and officer transition for fraternities and sororities.

In this book—*From Letters to Leaders: Redefining New Member Education and Leveraging Belonging to Eliminate Hazing*—we recognized that in order to fix some of the problems we see in news articles all over the country involving fraternities and sororities, we must carefully examine the new member education process. It all starts there, and

I believe this book will be helpful to college students, college administrators, alumni volunteers, and also national fraternity/sorority headquarters. We will spend some time talking about why the status quo is not sustainable, and then we will start to develop ideas on how to address some of these issues.

Students and administrators who are not affiliated typically don't understand the differences in Greek Letter Organizations (GLOs), and typically don't understand the differences in all the councils either. It's important for us to start by explaining the history of the fraternal movement and why it matters when solving some of these issues. There are local Greek Letter Organizations that do not have a headquarters to rely on for help in building a good new member education program. There are many GLOs that are largely run by alumni without full-time professional staff to assist. Even within the larger national fraternities and sororities, there can be inconsistencies in terms of the new member education process between chapters. All of these organizations must work together to provide more consistency within the new member education experience. If there is one organization on campus that fails to deliver, this could negatively impact all organizations on campus. This book will help to identify areas to focus on for new member education that is constructive and effective without hazing new members.

There is often a mentality of "earning your letters" for new members of fraternities and sororities, that we should make it difficult for the new member, otherwise they won't appreciate their membership and/or value the organization. I have two problems with this line of thinking. First, I often deal with a significant amount of apathy in college fraternities and sororities, and that increases over time to the point where senior members of the fraternity/sorority are completely disengaged from the chapter, which then leads to an alumnus who disappears completely. Could it be that this process of "earning your letters" makes the student feel like they have crossed the finish line after their difficult new member process, and now they can coast for the next three years? Would it be better for us to create a new member education process that is actually four years long, and have different educational programs each year to satisfy the changing needs of the student as they approach senior year, and then they become fully initiated members in the fraternity/sorority upon graduation with their degree? Perhaps in their freshman year we focus more on history of the organization and the chapter, and by senior year the content has shifted over time to now be focused on networking and interviewing skills for a job. Their needs shift over time, and our fraternity/sorority membership education needs to also shift accordingly. Why do we often stop teaching after freshman year? Aren't we doing a disservice to our members? If we have problems with retention of our members over time, this is a good way to keep all of our members engaged through graduation.

My second issue with "earning your letters" is that it's not in line with the origin of fraternities and sororities. As the first chapter will outline for you, fraternities started as an extension of debate and literary societies. There are values associated with these organizations, and the fraternity would be a place that members would commit to these shared values. The founders of our organizations, both nationally and locally at your university, never went through any hazing to get admission into the organization. I meet members of the fraternity I joined in college every week, from all over the country. Sometimes they are twenty years younger than I am. Sometimes they are twenty years older than I am. Sometimes they joined in New York. Sometimes they joined in California. I would never ask them to prove to me that they are a member of the fraternity by cleaning my house. I would never ask them to finish a fifth of alcohol in order to prove to me that they are a member of the fraternity. If they live their lives in accordance with our shared values in the fraternity, then they are a member. Hopefully, if we are doing recruitment the right way, we should be proactively inviting members into our fraternity based on the fact that they have already displayed our values on the outside. By committing to recruiting 365 days a year, we can observe potential new members over time and find out if they truly believe in the values of our organization. If we only commit to "rush" the first two weeks of each semester, then we have a harder time observing our values in the potential new members. In that scenario of "rush," we might be making errors in terms of who we invite into the organization, so it's time to think about changing the structure of both recruitment and new member education.

As you start to think about your own new member education process, I would encourage you to think about what Gen Z is really looking for, as opposed to what we've always done in the past. The new member education processes of the past were geared toward different generations and different needs that may not resonate with Gen Z. If our goal is recruitment and retention of Gen Z students, then we need to be open to doing new member education slightly different than the way you experienced it. In working with Gen Z every day of my life (both the college students on college campuses and my two children who will be attending college in the next 2–3 years), they all want a CUSTOMIZED experience. For example, look at the branding on Instagram for Gen Z students. It's all very customized and individualized in terms of colors and style to the student. They have their own brand. Same thing is true for the new member experience. Today's students want it to be customized to their skills and their needs, not the same, generic experience for every new member that has come through in the last one hundred years.

This is a good time to be clear with the new members on the expectations of membership (a one-page syllabus with the potential new member signature is helpful) that outlines things such as GPA requirements, study hours, length of the new member program, an alcohol-free experience, involvement in other organizations on campus to encourage the growth of your fraternity/sorority, and the amount/collection dates of dues/initiation fees. Follow up here with your organization's anti-hazing statement.

We can look at new member education in eight sections, which could easily correspond to eight weeks, or eight days. In creating this customized new member education experience, start with the history of the organization and the chapter. Try to make the history relevant to today, and having an alumnus of the chapter to tell the story might be helpful in making it relevant to the students and engaging in a two-way dialogue—whether that be in person or on video conferencing. Next up would be academics/scholarship, and you can lean on the Greek University resources here for time management and study skills, as well as peer mentoring study groups within the chapter. A section on brotherhood/sisterhood is helpful next to promote teambuilding and *chapter* unity—notice I didn't say "pledge class" unity. It's important to build the bonds of brotherhood/sisterhood throughout the entire chapter in order to be effective. We don't want four cliques within your chapter because it's not an effective way to run an organization. Risk management and awareness education would come next (policies from the university, your organization), which would include things such as sexual assault prevention, alcohol/drug abuse prevention, hazing prevention, men's health awareness, and diversity/inclusion programming. Next I would move to community service and planning for a chapter event to give back to the community. Leadership could come next where we implement a shadowing program with chapter officers so the new members know exactly what they do and how to do it once the current chapter officers graduate. A logical next step would be the values of the organization, and having chapter members share what the organization means to them. Finally, alumni networking and initiation. This is a good opportunity for the new members to get to know the alumni that are in their field of study, correspond with them by phone or email, and start to open lines of communication that will help the new members get the internships/jobs they will need in the future.

This book will be a valuable guide to help you understand some of the things that should be considered when going through new member education. If we can start our new members off on the right foot with education that is customized to their specific needs, I believe we can *recruit better and retain better* going forward. Should you need any of the chapter authors on your campus to speak on these areas directly with the fraternity/sorority community, please let me know and we'll be very happy to make that happen for you. I believe in you!

"There is divine beauty in learning. To learn means to accept the postulate that life did not begin at my birth. Others have been here before me, and I walk in their footsteps." —Elie Wiesel

Michael can be reached by email at: bookings@greekuniversity.org

The website is: www.greekuniversity.org

CHAPTER 1

Alpha to Omega:
The Power of Sankofa in a Brief History of Collegiate Greek Letter Organizations (GLOs)

Tish Norman, M. Ed

The Writer's "Why"

I have spent close to twenty years supporting fraternity/ sorority communities by teaching success strategies, how to attract ideal candidates, leadership development, successful recruitments, DE&I (Diversity, Equity, & Inclusion), council history, culture and traditions. As an affiliated member, I have lived the highs *and lows* of fraternity/sorority life, and the advantages and disadvantages of membership. However, it wasn't until I became a historian of Greek Life, that I really began researching the *history* of the fraternal movement. As a sorority woman and consultant in this game for over fifteen years, I know the culture. Well, I thought I did. Real talk . . . it wasn't until **I was intentional about researching the history that my understanding increased.**

My questions are:

- What do you *really* know about your organization . . . not chapter, but organization?
- Does the history matter?
- Does the history matter to *you*?
- Do you want to learn more than what you currently know?
- Why is fraternal history important?

I want to inspire you to learn more. No matter the organization or council, we are interconnected. We share "relatable" experiences, cultural exchanges, and similar objectives—in some form or another. As you conduct your own self-study, recruit new members, introduce your organization to your campus, or facilitate new-member education, remember to approach it with a conscious, equitable, and inclusive mindset. Use my chapter as a starting point to support such work.

After this chapter, readers will:

1. Better understand paradigms of social, personal, and organizational identity
2. Learn the origins of Fraternity and Sorority Life

3. Gain historical perspectives relating to contemporary issues
4. Feel an increased sense of belonging within FSL
5. Better understand the circumstances in which the organizations and councils were formed
6. Build knowledge of the intended understanding of the Sankofa principle

Time is but a fleeting moment. It is transitory. As American hymn writer Jennie Bain Wilson wrote, "Time is filled with swift transition." There are some moments, however, that stand out, influence the culture, shape thought, define decades, and can make us feel like time actually stood still. The following chapter is an introduction to a few of those moments—moments that shaped a culture and defined a history, spanning some 245 years.

Where and How Did GLOs Begin?

Fraternity and Sorority Life, FSL, is known as a social establishment that was designed to foster the learning and development of college students who affiliate with social fraternities and sororities. While the FSL experience can provide developmental opportunities for its members, it is important to note that this American institution is not void of serious challenges . . . since the beginning. The culture is fascinating and treacherous.

American college Greek-letter societies are a unique development of American collegians and every year, roughly 750,000+ students spend time in these organizations. Sadly, these groups have also been troubled with racism, sexism, violence, sexual assault, hazing, alcohol and drug abuse, recklessness, psychological manipulation, and many other challenges. *So, where and how did it all begin?* The reoccurring theme that always resurfaces is that members lacked a fundamental understanding of fraternal history—a history that is complex and often difficult to hear.

Today, fraternal organizations are affiliated with governing bodies that either oversee all modes of operation or that provides organizational support. The Interfraternity Council (IFC), established in 1909, represents 57 inter/national all-men's fraternities. Historically, these have been majority Anglo male members. Founded in 1902, the National Panhellenic Conference (NPC) is the governing body for more than 375, 000 members in 26 inter/national women-only social organizations. Historically, these groups have been comprised of majority Anglo women. The National Pan-Hellenic Council (NPHC), was formed in 1930 to unite its 9 fraternity and sorority member organizations, which historically, were predominantly African-American. The Multicultural Greek Council (NMGC), was founded in 1998, supporting 10 male and female member groups. This governing body promotes all aspects of multiculturalism among its organizations.

Finally, as a Pan-African research scholar, I took the liberty of incorporating the metaphorical symbol, "Sankofa," traditionally used by the Akan people of Ghana, to provide an allegorical link that stresses the importance of knowing one's history. Sankofa teaches us that we should use our past to guide us, so we can move forward with confidence. The Sankofa symbol is a bird whose legs are facing forward, while its head is turning backwards to eat an egg. This symbolizes the integration of the wisdom of the past to inform and build the future.

Sankofa literally means, "go back and get it," and the Akan people believed that there is wisdom in learning from the past. In the same way, for contemporary FSL groups to better understand themselves and the implications of the fraternal movement, we will start at the beginning. Alpha.

Interfraternity Council (IFC)

Prior to thirteen years ago, I possessed very little knowledge about the history of traditionally Anglo fraternal organizations. My lived experiences with these groups were non-existent and my limited perception had basically been shaped by stereotypes. I am a Black woman that attended a Black college, and affiliated friends and family were members of Black fraternal organizations. This was all I knew. My worldview was informed by the Black experience, so generally speaking, I knew nothing. Teen comedies like *Revenge of the Nerds* and *Animal House* showcased stereotypical depictions of these groups but still . . . I didn't know much.

Over the past ten years, as I began connecting with these groups and conducting deeper research into the Black fraternal movement, I knew that in order to gain a more comprehensive understanding of Black fraternal culture, I needed to research the origins of this entire movement. Surely, I could not base my knowledge on Hollywood movies, right? How did these organizations start? Where? When? What time period?

The institution of US college Greek Letter Organizations is truly a unique development of the American college student. Greek Life emerged in the 1700s as an extension of debate teams and literary societies. During this era, college life was intentionally patterned after that of the European system of higher education, as apparent in the academics, campus life, religious associations, and even building structure. The handful of American colleges were designed to prepare middle-class Anglo males for the clergy, so social activities were non-existent.

By the mid-eighteenth century, there were nine colleges in the colonial states, and the first male fraternity started in 1776, with the formation of Phi Beta Kappa at the College of William & Mary in Williamsburg, Virginia.[1] This group

---

[1]   Matthew W. Hughey, "Rushing the Wall, Crossing the Sands: Cross-Racial Membership in US College Fraternities and Sororities," in Craig L.

had all of the elements of many modern fraternities—a key or badge, Greek mottos, vows of secrecy, Greek letters, rituals, a secret handshake, and an initiation. According to greekyearbook.com, one of the PBK organizers was a Greek scholar, and began naming college organizations after the PBK secret motto. Other than literary societies and debate clubs, student groups were prohibited, so this development was monumental. Birthed out of a desire for a student's need for connectedness and fellowship, the American fraternity, which derives from the Latin *Frater* meaning "brother" was formed.

American colleges and universities were designed for and thrived on progress, preparation, and development of affluent white male students only. College life was pretty homogeneous, as women and people of color were not a part of this landscape. In spite of this, many students were impressed with the idea of close fraternal organizations as several GLOs sprang up on many campuses over the next few decades.

High ideals like honor, leadership, academic excellence, fellowship, and service were common pillars that fraternity life aspired to embody. I am inclined to believe that there was a period when fraternity men lead the charge of service, philanthropy, and achievement. By the time the Interfraternity Council was founded in 1909, its mission was clear—to foster a healthy and vibrant fraternity community.

Torbenson and Gregory S. Parks, *Brothers and Sisters: Diversity in College Fraternities and Sororities* (Cranbury, NJ: Rosemont Publishing, 2009), 237–76.

The opportunities to form positive, enriching fraternal bonds were endless.

College life ceased during the Civil War, as many colleges closed and several fraternities became disconnected. After the war, southern colleges witnessed a rebirth of fraternity life as thirteen new fraternities were founded. Many of these organizations were poorly run, having no account of records, designated places to gather, or no centralized national body to unite the growing numbers of chapters. Slowly, one of the developments that became very common was the talk of owning a club room or chapter house for members to reside.

As an influx of students continued into the nineteenth century, chapters continued to grow and the need for housing was a concern. Soon, the fraternity house became a staple in Greekdom. According to Nicholas Syrett, the University of California, Berkeley was home to the first frat house in 1876, and by 1920, some 774 houses had been erected.[2] This way, colleges were able to enroll more students and a golden era of American college life was beginning to take flight. For a short time, these groups served with more purpose, but with the rapid growth of students and the arrival of women students, a gamut of issues quickly arose.

Consistently, adequate housing became the least of the worries for fraternity members. Fraternity life had not only been criticized since its inception, but by the mid-twentieth century, this entire institution was being defined by middle-

---

[2]   Nicholas Syrett, *The Company He Keeps: A History of White College Fraternities* (Chapel Hill, NC: University of North Carolina Press, 2009), 207.

class Protestant white males consolidating power on campus, riddled with excessive drinking, sexually humiliating hazing, hazardous initiations, high rates of sexual assault, and fatal accidents.[3]

Let me be clear: this is not a bashing of historically white social fraternities. It is evident that they offer leadership development opportunities and members have benefitted from affiliation. However, when "fraternity life" traditionally becomes synonymous with incessantly risky behavior and structurally racist legacies, the continued relevancy of these groups must be examined. IFC fraternities have a unique responsibility to use their privilege to educate, positively influence, and make situations better. Fraternity offers opportunities for success, and being a part of this culture increases one's chances at attaining high levels of achievement. If historically white social fraternities would resist old behaviors and dangerous stereotypes in exchange for anti-racist ideology and more constructive engagement, then, not only would the world see less tragedy and more added value, but Greek Life would be visible everywhere.

For more information, visit: https://nicfraternity.org/

---

[3]   Lisa Wade, "Why Colleges Should Get Rid of Fraternities for Good," *TIME*, May 19, 2017, https://time.com/4784875/fraternities-timothy-piazza/.

National Panhellenic Conference (NPC)

Established 1902

In studying Panhellenic sorority women, I have discovered that there is limited research available on this topic. While scholarly research has been conducted on both sororities and fraternities on various matters, pertaining to sororities, the lack of research is an indication of the need of more scholarly attention turned toward this topic. The following incorporates factual information from a variety of quality sources that supports this knowledge.

A change had come! After the Civil War, the American college system underwent massive growth and expansion. In the late nineteenth century and early twentieth century, Greek societies experienced phenomenal growth as veterans and Anglo women began entering college in large numbers. Many women sought community with one another, as they were outnumbered and desired something of their own. The first secret society founded for collegiate women was the Adelphean Society, now Alpha Delta Pi. This organization was established in 1851 at Wesleyan Female College in Macon, Georgia.[4]

---

[4]   https://wesleyancollege.libguides.com/archives/alphadeltapi

Women's fraternities, which quickly became known as women's sororities, were inspired by and patterned after the rapid expansion of Greek fraternities across the nation. Sorority, like fraternity, derives from the Latin word *Soror* meaning "sister," and was deemed more appropriate than fraternity. Some of these groups also stemmed from the growth of literary societies, as these were student groups that promoted ethical conduct, scholarship, and were very popular during this era.

From the time the American college system was established, most colleges had literary societies. To reiterate, American college Greek Letter Organizations helped fill the social needs of the early college student, who, once again, were white middle-class men. As more women's secret societies were established across the country, women began organizing themselves to bring more meaning to their campus life. Like their male counterparts, they began bearing Greek-letter names, Greek mottos, oaths of secrecy, colors, rituals, seals, badges, secret handshakes, and initiation rites. Founders of these sororities recognized the importance of unifying women in the name of fellowship and forming relationships while at college. On a deeper level, ideals like improvement, scholarship, and personal development were promoted, so many like-minded women were naturally drawn.

Like every group being discussed in this chapter, traditionally white female GLOs faced their fair share of challenges as well. Through the years, threats of hazing, sexual assault, and alcohol poisoning have contributed to systemic problems. Recruitment week or "rush week," can also be challenging for a number of reasons. Recruitment is the time fraternities and sororities recruit student to join their respective organizations. Though groups have slightly different practices, it all involves getting (mostly) incoming freshman to learn more about Greek Life. Over time, this practice quickly evolved into fierce competition.

Traditionally, as sorority housing became more common, organizations needed to fill their beds, and these groups literally "rushed" to recruit what appeared to be the best and brightest incoming students.[5] This was very prominent among early social sororities and drew the attention of faculty and administration. According to Amy Wells, in an effort to limit such interference, and for the purpose of "cooperating with college administration, so high standards are maintained throughout the whole college," the National Panhellenic Conference was formed in 1902.[6] This was the first governing body to be established out of all collegiate GLOs.

NPC sorority women today are still fantastic! They are spirited and are excellent leaders . . . but still struggle with often chaotic protocol governing recruitment week. Active members not only have to balance hosting parties and events in order to meet upwards of 1,000 "potential new members," or PNMs, but must do so diplomatically. Real talk . . . the competition can get nasty. Every group feels the pressure of wanting to recruit the best PNMs, and often times, the focus

---

[5]   Christopher Geno, "What Is Rush?" *Campus Explorer*, 2021, https://www.campusexplorer.com/college-advice-tips/4B209587/What-is-Rush/.

[6]   Amy E. Wells, "Sororities," in *Women in Higher Education: An Encyclopedia*, ed. Ana M. Martínez Alemán and Kristen A. Renn (Santa Barbara, CA: ABC-CLIO, Inc., 2002).

seems to be on how lavish and extravagant the events are rather than the compatibility of future sisters.

Despite all of the challenges that arise among sorority-affiliated women, more and more women are going Greek. Greek Life would not be what it is today without the visionary, talented, and purpose-driven Panhellenic woman. My hope is for your affiliate organizations' continued incorporation of your missions into your daily lives as well as furthering new initiatives so women may continue to be impacted of this movement. National Panhellenic Conference sororities rising!

For more information, visit: https://www.npcwomen.org/

National Pan-Hellenic Council (NPHC)

I have to give it to you, straight, no chaser. Black people were enslaved in America while traditionally white fraternal groups thrived on US college campuses. When slavery was abolished in 1863, not only had male fraternities been in existence for over eighty-five years, but the first National Panhellenic Conference sorority had also been established in 1851.[7] Racism in fraternity life dates back to the beginning

---

[7]   Nadine Jolie Courtney, "Which Sorority Was Actually the First?" *Town & Country*, May 18, 2017, https://www.townandcountrymag.com/society/tradition/a9660538/first-oldest-college-sorority/#:~:text=The%20First%20

of its founding, and while white fraternities and sororities expanded, strict government policies and institutional practices fueled systemic racism, which included prohibiting Black Americans from attending PWIs, predominantly white institutions.

At the turn of the twentieth century, Black Americans faced insurmountable hardships, based on segregation and racial inequality. Few managed to attend PWIs, but were not permitted access to residential housing, campus life, and of course, joining fraternal organizations. Sadly, these types of restrictive activities reflected what was not just the societal norm, but the campus norm. Through the ratification of the 14th Amendment in 1868, PWIs saw a slow increase in enrollment from students of color, and liberal universities like Oberlin College (Ohio), Berea College (Kentucky), Cornell University (New York), and Washington & Lee University (Virginia) were admitting and educating Black students. Others found their "home away from home" at Black colleges, which had been around since 1837. Since this time, historically Black colleges and universities (HBCUs) have truly added a unique and distinguishable chapter in the development of America's higher educational system.

Most private and public HBCUs were established in the mid 1800s, and many aspects of HBCU life afforded its students tremendous benefits. However, a truly distinguishing feature of HBCU culture—the Black fraternal movement—would not materialize for another seventy-five years. By the time HBCUs underwent rapid expansion, white fraternal groups had already

---

To%20Be%20Called%20%E2%80%9CSorority%E2%80%9D%3A%20 Gamma%20Phi%20Beta.

been in existence for over a century. To reiterate, handfuls of Black students were admitted to PWIs, but were ostracized—basically invisible. They faced extreme racism from professors and students in and outside of the classroom. Black students were conscious of their struggles on campus, and empathized with one another's need for community and social support.

The aforementioned is what makes the history of the Black fraternal movement one of great significance to the annals of history. Inspired by Black political and social justice movements, along with support from the local Black community, a gathering of Black male Cornell University students began meeting as an off-campus study and social club. As a result of these gatherings, the Black Greek-letter fraternal movement began in 1906, with the founding of the first Black intercollegiate fraternity, Alpha Phi Alpha. In 1908, Alpha Kappa Alpha became the first Black sorority, established at Howard University.

Over the next sixteen years, BGLOs, which became known by many as the "Elite Eight," were established. Five of the then eight were founded at Howard University, monikered, "The Mecca." Following the footsteps of Alpha Phi Alpha and Alpha Kappa Alpha, successive BGLOs were founded upon similar principles of achievement, scholarship, betterment and service. These groups revolutionized student life for Black students everywhere.

Surviving Jim Crow and the Civil Rights Movement, these organizations continued their plights to serve its members and communities. Inspired by the sociopolitical climate of the 1960s, Iota Phi Theta became the ninth and final BGLO, as its members were heavily involved in the social justice work of the time. They carried themselves as such. Distinguishable cultural traits quickly arose, as BGLOs developed distinct styles and personalities. Influenced by an amalgamation of African cultural performance, militaristic cadences, and Black American customs, BGLOs' presence was felt by their slides, glides, songs, and strolls. Each group developed unique stomp and clap routines, with large and powerful movements. Some preferred precision or more fluid shifts in movement, while others step, hop and leap, similar to calisthenics.

These cultural performative presentations were exhilarating and extravagant, to say the least. Elaborate yard shows, step shows, colors, chants, and song circles were idiosyncratic to Black Greeks. Beginning in the late 1920s, each organization cultivated accoutrement, hand signs, calls, and programs that were distinct to them. The culture and tradition were very vibrant and spirited. HBCUs were epicenters for this cultural phenomenon, and for close to one hundred years, BGLOs have used this performative expression to initiate new members, sing chants about their history, fundraise, introduce new members, showcase their creativity, and celebrate the brotherhood and sisterhood.

This institution, however, did not come without its fair share of struggle and complexities. Besides racial tension and prejudice students at PWIs faced, Black Greek life at HBCUs struggled with institutionalized racism, chauvinism, relevant programming, fatal hazing processes, and brutal initiations. Sadly, these and a plethora of other complex issues have plagued these organizations for decades. Despite their governing body's interventions, the struggle continues. Much scholarship has been dedicated to increase the sustainability of these organizations, and while progress to eradicate these complexities has improved, there is still much reformation needed.

Arguably, the last 115 years are better because of the Black fraternal movement. The aid, support, and civic-minded direction that BGLOs have provided for the Black collegian is incomparable. This institution, like no other, has positively impacted over 1.5 million members internationally, with prominent membership to include Dr. Martin Luther King Jr., Shaquille O'Neal, Aretha Franklin, Colin Kaepernick, and US Vice-President, Kamala Harris. With the proper support, guidance, and high-quality members, the impact of National Panhellenic organizations will be felt for another century and more.

For more information, visit:
https://nphchq.com/millennium1/

National Multicultural Greek Council (NMGC)

Like the National Pan-Hellenic Council, the National Multicultural Greek Council (NMGC) consists of both fraternities and sororities. Established in 1998, multicultural fraternal organizations have also answered a unique call for the members in which they serve. Various dimensions of diversity and cultural identities like ethnicity, nationality, sexual orientation, geographical location, and religious beliefs are all fundamental aspects of multiculturalism that have become more prominent in the last fifty years. To answer the call of the greater community-at-large, these groups have developed a tradition of providing support and service to its constituent organizations in very special ways.

All culturally-based fraternal organizations (CBFOs) share similar histories, as the racist exclusionary practices of the traditionally white fraternities/sororities, along with the absence of substantive support networks for marginalized students, led students of color to seek refuge in these organizations. However, slightly different from BGLOs, whose membership was predominantly Black students, CBFOs served their membership up with a twist. Let's explore.

International students enrolled in US colleges as early as the 1700s. In 1889, the short-lived Latin American fraternity, Alpha Zeta, that was mainly comprised of international Latin American students was founded at Cornell University. Though some were short-lived, chapters like Alpha Lambda Mu at the University of Pennsylvania date back over 100 years, as it was from 1889 to 1949 that Latin American and Asian and Pacific Islander fraternal groups really took their place.

These organizations, mostly comprised of international students studying in the US, enhanced race pride, and began developing their own customs and traditions, which promoted friendship and cooperation among group members. As immigration policies became more relaxed in the early twentieth century, multiculturalism began increasing in various regions across the country. Naturally, campuses saw an uptick in CBFOs. Rho Psi, the first Asian-American fraternity was founded in 1916 at Cornell University. On the US West Coast, where the Asian-American population was increasing, Asian organizations began surfacing, beginning with Pi Alpha Pi fraternity (founded in 1926 at the University of California, Berkley), Chi Alpha Delta sorority (founded in 1928 at the University of California, Los Angeles), and Sigma Omicron Phi sorority (founded at San Francisco State Teachers' College in 1930).

Over the next several years, CBFOs witnessed a gamut of outcomes. Some campuses saw gradual expansion and growth as chapters were established at PWIs like Lehigh University (Pennsylvania), Louisiana State University, and Kansas State University. These groups were not common at HBCUs, as those institutions predominantly served students of African descent. According to Oliver Fajardo, many of these groups were defunct by the early 1970s, but Asian Greek fraternity, Pi Alpha Phi, records that advances in technology and an explosion in Asian American students during the 1970s and 1980s helped "usher in a fast-growing population."[8] Not

---

[8]   Oliver Fajardo, "History of Latino Fraternal Movement and Why It Matters," April 2015, https://cdn.ymaws.com/www.afa1976.org/resource/collection/ABDB5914-1754-4B8A-A477-DD4130EA781E/Farjardo_April_2015_-_Researcher.pdf.

only that, but the desire to highlight cultures and qualities of multicultural students rose to the forefront of student needs as well.

While all national organizations have removed traditional discriminatory practices, many nuances still linger. Beyond that as well as racially-insensitive chapter chants, IFC fraternities' cross-racial membership has become more diversified over the years. The same applies to Panhellenic organizations that extend more bids to potential new members of culturally diverse backgrounds. Matthew Hughey wrote that non-Black members have been a part of Black Greek organizations as early as the mid 1940s, but what truly sets CBFOs apart from other groups is that a majority of their member organizations value *all cultures*.[9] According to https://nationalmgc.org/, multicultural organizations do not concentrate on one aspect of culture, but rather embrace and regard one's "individuality as the foundation of unity."

The growing number of Hispanic, Asian, American Indian, and Pacific Islander GLOs significantly increased in the 1970s and 80s. This came during the era of the Civil Rights and Black Power movements, as social justice and student movements from BIPOC (Black Indigenous People of Color) were in full swing, bringing more of these populations to US campuses.[10] A majority of CBFOs membership is from Latin descent, so pillars like race pride, a sense of belonging, and cultural awareness continue to be foundational principles of success.

---

[9]   Hughey, "Crossing the Sands," 259.
[10] Fajardo, "History of Latino Fraternal Movement."

Today, these groups are more popular today than ever. Despite many of the organizations phasing out, CBFOs continue to exist to address the growing needs of multicultural students through new charters and relevant interactions. Developmental and social needs, similar to that of Panhellenic sororities for white female students and BGLOs for Black students, was targeted toward students of color who recognized that the promotion of community, social engagement and friendships among multicultural students was at hand. What exciting futures these groups have before them. Remain relevant. The future needs you.

For more information, visit: https://nationalmgc.org/

The National Association of Latino Fraternal Organizations, Inc. (NALFO)

By now, we have learned historical aspects about the larger fraternity and sorority councils, and it is not over yet. As our country continues to grow and Greek Life continues to impact the lives of American college students, so does the need to diversify the burgeoning organizations that serve these populations. Throughout the chapter, I have highlighted activities like *rush, recruitment,* and *intake,* as terms that various councils use to bring in new members to their organizations. Intake is the term most commonly used by NPHC and CBFOs, so let us highlight another council that is making an impact on campuses across the U.S.

Established in 1998, The National Association of Latino Fraternal Organizations, Inc. (NALFO) is the premier umbrella council to its sixteen-member organizations. NALFO is unique in its existence, as this governing body exhibits the potential of and highlights one united Latino Greek front. We know that all Greek councils serve as support networks for their member organizations, and one of the unique characteristics of NALFO is that their mission is motivated by their affiliate organizations' desire to build community amongst themselves, for enhanced chapter experiences, and having a sense of belonging within the larger FSL.

What's unique about the affiliate organizations is their small chapter sizes and how they are structured. Every chance I get to speak to audiences where NALFO chapters are present, I remind them of their unique positioning. As a growing council, yes—you can be inspired by leadership of IFC, the organization of NPC, the distinctiveness of NPHC, and the boldness of NMGC. There is a connectedness among all councils that links us through common goals, traditions, and objectives. However, as each group has done before you, NALFO has the opportunity to develop your own unique space in FSL. Let me encourage you to continue to make your own mark.

The heritage that NALFO chapters carry with them daily should be the foundation of their unique presence on campus. This council was formed to provide community and support for Latinos on campus. When you sense that you matter, feel accepted and respected among yourselves, and feel valued and seen, that truly makes a difference. NALFO has the potential to be strong and mighty. At the core, this is what NALFO embodies—a relevant cultural community, where like-minded peers foster and promote interfraternal connections.

For more information, visit: https://nalfo.org/

National APIDA Panhellenic Council (NAPA)

Greek Life continues to reverberate across the country. As we know, the presence of culturally-based Greek organizations goes back to the early twentieth century, and the presence of international students attending US colleges dates back to the eighteenth century. Despite the struggles with small numbers and sustainability, among other challenges, since the 1920s, students of color have benefitted from the presence of cultural Greek organizations on campus.

When considering the Black Indigenous People of Color (BIPOC) populations in FSL, the absence of the Asian/Pacific Islander population, in the broader scope, does not lend to the inclusive objective many campuses have today. So, I will seize this opportunity to highlight the still, relatively young South-Asian fraternities and sororities that make up NAPA.

These organizations' presence began in 1992 with the founding of the first South Asian sorority, Delta Phi Beta, at the University of California, Berkeley.[11] Prior to the growing numbers that we see today, Latinx Greek-letter and Asian Greek-letter organizations really began to gain momentum during the 1970s and 1980s.[12] The Asian population is significantly diverse, so to acknowledge communities within this community, so to speak, the acronym APIDA, coined by Dr. Mamta Accapadi, encompasses Asian/Pacific Islander/Desi-Americans.[13]

Other than normal FSL culture, the unique traditions and customs that are woven in the fabric of the NPHC, NMGC, NALFO, IFC and NPC organizations have, some NAPA groups have adopted similar cultural affects like hand signs, colors, "crossing garments," performative presentations, stepping, strolling, and call.[14] All of this works together to promote awareness of Asian heritage on campus and beyond. One of the characteristics that NAPA boasts that will carry them into the future is how organizations with different

---

[11] Bilal Badruddin, "Lions, Tigers, and South Asian Greeks: Oh, My! The Opportunity for More Research!" *Texas Education Review* Vol. 5, Issue 2 (2017).

[12] Susana M. Muñoz and Juan R. Guardia, "Nuestra historia y futuro (our history and future): Latino/a fraternities and sororities," in *Brothers and Sisters: Diversity in College Fraternities and Sororities*, 104–32.

[13] Badruddin, "Lions, Tigers, and South Asian Greeks."

[14] Walter M. Kimbrough, *Black Greek 101: The Culture, Customs, and Challenges of Black Fraternities and Sororities* (Madison, NJ: Fairleigh Dickinson University Press, 2003).

beliefs, traditions, and cultures can come together in order to become something greater than they are separately.

For more information, visit: https://napahq.org/

For better or for worse, each year thousands of young coeds seek membership in Greek Letter Organizations. If there were not clear benefits, these organizations would not have prospered for centuries. Being affiliated with these groups fosters leadership development, feelings of belonging, and lifelong bonds. Though often controversial, social fraternities and sororities enhance the educational environment.

As an active and financial sorority woman, I am here to remind you that you cannot know where you are going unless you know where you have been. It is for this reason that the foundation of this book started with a brief history and this chapter began by introducing the meaning of Sankofa— the significant histories; the foundation of our beloved organizations. "You must reach back to reclaim that which is lost in order to move forward." New initiates, advisors, seasoned members, parents, and stakeholders alike—it is my hope that you, too, are inspired to be a researcher of fraternal history, from the beginning until . . . Omega.

Further Reading

African American Fraternities and Sororities: The Legacy and the Vision, Tamara L. Brown, Gregory S. Parks, and Clarenda M. Phillips

A Pledge with Purpose: Black Sororities and Fraternities and the Fight for Equality, Gregory S. Parks and Matthew W. Hughey

Black Greek 101: The Culture, Customs and Challenges of Black Fraternities and Sororities, Walter Kimbrough

Black Haze: Violence, Sacrifice, and Manhood in Black Greek-Letter Fraternities, Ricky Jones

Blackballed: The Black and White Politics of Race on America's Campuses, Lawrence Ross

Bound by a Mighty Vow: Sisterhood and Women's Fraternities, Diana Turk

Brothers and Sisters: Diversity in College Fraternities and Sororities, Craig L. Torbenson and Gregory S. Parks

Foundations, Research, and Assessment of Fraternities and Sororities: Retrospective and Future Considerations, Pietro Sasso et al.

Inside Greek U: Fraternities, Sororities, and the Pursuit of Pleasure, Power, and Prestige, Alan D. DeSantis

Moving Culturally-Based Sororities and Fraternities Forward: Innovations in Practice, Crystal Garcia and Antonio Duran

Pledged: The Secret Life of Sororities, Alexandra Robbins

Supporting Fraternities and Sororities in the Contemporary Era, Pietro Sasso et al.

The Company He Keeps: A History of White College Fraternities, Nicholas Syrett

Wrongs of Passage: Fraternities, Sororities, Hazing, and Binge Drinking, Hank Newer

Tish Norman is a native of Cleveland, Ohio, and is the Executive Director of Transforming Leaders Now, Inc., an educational consulting company specializing in college and career readiness, women's leadership, and the African-American experience.

Tish started her career in the classroom in Cincinnati, Ohio, teaching 3rd and 4th grade, and after being crowned Miss Black Cincinnati, she decided to take her gifts to Hollywood. Commercials, music videos, game shows, documentaries, sitcoms, Tish did it all!

After ten years of grinding in Hollywoodland, guess where Tish ended up? Yup, you're right! Back in the classroom. Out of an amalgamation of all of her professional experiences in education, pageantry, and acting, one day, Tish found her sweet spot: on stage, delivering a keynote to 500 high school students . . . and loved it!

Now, almost twenty years later, as a professional speaker and having delivered over 1,000 presentations, Tish's unparalleled energy, delivery style, and stirring keynotes have become favorites among universities, associations, and leadership conferences from coast to coast.

Tish is a contributing author of several articles and three books, *From Mediocre to Magnificent*, *Leading the Way*, and the newly released, *BLACKOUT: Real Issues and Real Solutions to Real Challenges Facing Black Student Affairs Professionals.*

A graduate of Kentucky State University, Tish has a Master's in Education from Pepperdine University and is a doctoral pursuant in Pan-African Studies, where her research focuses on memory and the Black sorority.

Having spoken in 45 states and 14 countries and despite her rigorous academic obligations, Tish still maintains an active speaking schedule, keynoting at dozens of campuses and leadership conferences every year. In 2017, Tish returned to her roots in Georgia and calls Atlanta home.

You can see Tish's programs at: www.greekuniversity.org/tish

Email Tish: tish@greekuniversity.org

CHAPTER 2

A Perversion of Greek Culture:
The Decline of Healthy New Member Processes

Joseph Thompson

When I joined my fraternity in 2007, it was an amazing experience. As new members, we spent most of our time getting to know one another. We learned the history, values, and the "ins and outs" of the organization—from organizational functions and processes, to what makes a successful chapter. We engaged in service projects and philanthropic activities. We met with alumni and faculty and staff at the university. Our new member process felt just like a college orientation. We were given letters to wear from day one . . . which was a big deal for us. In our fraternity we are given the rights and privileges of membership at the time of bid acceptance, regardless of not being initiated yet. Our new member program was not viewed as a weeding out process, because the philosophy was if the chapter did the work to recruit the right people, they already justified our membership.

Attitude is everything. If you're a chapter recruiting new members and you take that process seriously, you should *only* be offering membership to people who you know will live your organization's values and put in the work to make your chapter more successful. If you need to use the new member period to weed people out, you didn't do your due diligence in recruiting the right people.

For those who don't know the history of *pledging*, this was a concept that most organizations moved away from over the past 30+ years. *Pledging* had a negative connotation. It was associated with the "weeding out" process and hazing. Most organizations replaced *pledging* with the *new member process* or *intake*. However, as we know, even though we can change the name and teach new concepts to a new generation of students, history will find a way to repeat itself. In some cases, new members must now be initiated in seventy-two hours; intake activities are heavily guarded by graduate chapters and advisors; campus officials collect detailed calendars—yet still these "underground" activities persist.

If we don't change the attitudes and beliefs of our members (and the alumni who influence us) about gaining membership, we won't change anything.

Most people probably don't even realize that the idea of pledging, new member program, or intake are entirely *relatively* new concepts. When most of our organizations were founded, they simply selected new members and initiated them. *Tapping* was a typical practice in which fraternities publicly tapped a prospective member on the shoulder and offered them membership. This of course was *after* they got to know these students and purposely chose them. There was no such thing as rush week.

So how did new member programs, pledging, or intake come about? And when did hazing become prevalent in our organizations?

Hazing has always existed on college campuses, but it was there long before fraternal organizations existed. In fact, one of the earliest known cases of hazing at a United States university was at Harvard in 1684, involving an upperclassman having new students perform acts of servitude and hitting them. Prior to the nineteenth century, hazing was typically associated with upperclassmen hazing underclassmen. It was the early 1800s when hazing found a new role within extracurricular student groups, and by the early 1900s it became so commonplace in fraternities that "Death at a Fraternity" was often in the headlines.[15] It was following World War II, however, when it became an epidemic.

After World War II, the G.I. Bill provided countless veterans the opportunity to attend college in the United States. Missing the camaraderie of their military service, there was a massive influx of men who joined fraternities. Post-Vietnam resulted in the same influx. It was after Vietnam, however,

---

[15] Hank Nuwer, *Broken Pledges: The Deadly Rite of Hazing* (Atlanta: Longstreet Press, 1990), 120.

when we saw alcohol really enter the mix, resulting in a staggering thirty-one hazing-related deaths in the 1970s.[16]

In 1972, with a goal to remove hazing culture in its chapters, Lambda Chi Alpha Fraternity became the first organization to remove the concept of pledging and replace it with *associate membership*. Associate membership allowed new members voting rights in chapter matters and the ability to run for officer positions, unlike other fraternities at the time. This is not to say they eradicated these behaviors but made a specific effort to reduce them by reducing power dynamics. Since then, many organizations have followed suit. In 1990, the National Pan-Hellenic Council, consisting of the Divine Nine, historically Black fraternities and sororities, banned pledging and moved to *membership intake*. Sigma Alpha Epsilon Fraternity updated their practices in 2014 to end pledging and move to a 72-hour initiation model. What prompted these big changes? High-profile hazing incidents in their organizations.

In total, over 200 university hazing deaths have occurred since 1838, with 40 deaths between 2007 and 2017 alone.[17] This is counting just deaths. How many incidents have occurred that luckily did not result in a death? How many incidents resulted in emotional and mental trauma that we haven't heard about? What about physical abuse? How did we even get here?

---

[16] Barbara B. Hollmann, "Hazing: Hidden Campus Crime," in *New Directions for Student Services*, Vol. 2002, Issue 99, pp. 11–24, https://onlinelibrary.wiley.com/doi/10.1002/ss.57.

[17] Hank Nuwer, *Hazing: Destroying Young Lives* (Bloomington, IN: Indiana University Press, 2018).

In my career I have worked with a great number of chapters, both as a volunteer and as a campus-based advisor. I have had to respond to a fraternity-related hazing incident more than once. Some of those chapters were high-functioning, award-winning chapters before or at the time. Some of those chapters were no more than five years old.

National organizations and campuses work diligently to educate our students on healthy, appropriate ways to orient our new members into our organizations. Certainly, no headquarters or university staff member is teaching students to haze. So, what makes a young chapter turn to these behaviors? What makes a chapter who seemingly does all the right things turn to harm rather than sticking with the healthy new member activities we teach them?

I believe it all starts with who and how we recruit.

I made the argument earlier that fraternities need to do a better job of recruiting men who live the organization's values. Once we shift our focus to recruiting men just because they're friends with us, or we have other things in common, or they are someone you could drink a beer with, we've lost the plot.

A quick story: I had a close friend in college who I shared an apartment with for a while. Of all the people I went to school with for four years, including my fraternity brothers, I spent the most time with him. We had many similar interests but were also incredibly different in a lot of ways. I was a campus leader and heavily involved, while he spent most of his time in his room napping and playing video games. When

I became a founding father of my chapter, he asked if I was going to try to recruit him. "No," I said. Why? Because even though he was one of my best friends, I knew him enough to know he wasn't going to be someone who contributed much to the organization. It was as simple as that. Not all my friends need to be my brothers, just as *not all my brothers need to be my friends.*

This is a concept that is difficult to grasp for many people. Why would I choose to spend time with people I am not friends with? Doesn't brotherhood/sisterhood *mean* friendship? If you ask me, yes and no. There is greater likelihood you are good friends with a handful of members in your chapter, but not *all* the members of your chapter. You joined because you enjoyed the friendships you built with a few people, and at least *liked* most of the other members.

I have seen this play out many ways. I have advised chapters who purposely stay small because they want *everyone* to be friends, and having only twenty members makes that manageable. There is a fear that if they became larger, they would lose the dynamic they have. Yes, they probably would, but if we really cared about the organization we belong to and what it stands for, wouldn't we want to share that with more people? On the flipside, there are chapters of 100+ members where some members hardly know one another. Guess what? That's okay! Sure, you should want to know all your brothers/sisters, but isn't the point of fraternity/sorority to better ourselves and better our community? Do we really need to be best friends with everyone to make that possible? Fraternity is a gift, and we should want to share that gift, even if it means not being friends with every single member of my chapter. If we all share common goals and values, isn't that what *really* matters?

So how do we know someone aligns with our values? Don't most college students join fraternities or sororities because they like the people? *Let's be honest.* Rarely does someone join a fraternity because they "like their values." I mean, I personally did, but I know that is not the norm. However, if we like a person as a potential member because you can see them in your chapter, someone similar to you, and YOU really believe in your organization's values, then that's easy math. If you're a service-oriented chapter and you meet someone who is committed to service, they might be a great candidate. It's really that easy. So, what if they are different than you in a lot of ways? There's strength in diversity. There are enough stereotypes about fraternities and sororities being homogenous. Stop contributing to them! The only thing that should truly matter is whether they will be positive contributors to the mission of the organization. Period.

I strongly believe that we as fraternity men and sorority women do not do our due diligence in recruiting the *right* members all the time. I know this might offend some of you, but it is the honest truth. You probably know it. And when we recruit members for the wrong reasons, we undermine who we say we are. Suddenly, ideas and behaviors that do not align with our organizational values begin to creep in. Rather than making decisions out of congruent values, love of brotherhood/ sisterhood, and service to others, we make decisions out of immaturity, or what is more fun, or for ego, or in the case of hazing—a conscious or unconscious thirst for power. *Hazers love that power differential.*

We will not always know who the hazers will be, but why not put in an effort to at least try? Before I was initiated, this was a part of our education. We were asked a lot of questions about our beliefs and had deep conversation about what it meant to join the fraternity. We talked specifically about expectations of the orientation process.

We titled this chapter using the term "perversion" on purpose. As chapters we often say we do one thing, and then do another. We alter from our intended course and distort the meaning of our values and ritual. How many chapters do we know (maybe our own) who talk about all the service we do, when in reality we maybe do a few hours a semester of legitimate service? How many of us talk about networking, but the only networking we do is over a beer in a fraternity house basement? We need to stop kidding ourselves and be honest with what we say and do. Not to mention that for hazing chapters, we sell this positive experience to potential members, only to turn around and basically *say you have to endure some negative experiences in order to get the positive ones.* How does that make any sense?

So if you want to ensure your chapter stays on the right path, it starts with recruitment. It starts with building relationships with students on your campus who you see living out the values of your organization. It means making it clear who you are and who you aren't and what behavior is acceptable and what is not. It continues with accountability in your chapter to ensure those beliefs grow and continue. Not everyone we recruit will be a Boy Scout, but they don't have to be. They just have to want to be better. We need to be honest with who we are and what we value. We need to stop selling one thing and then being another. When we do find the right members to join, we need to lift them up and treat them as equals. We need to treat our new member education like a college orientation. No hazing, just positive experiences that bring you all together, teach the history of the organization, and prepare your new members to be the next leaders of the chapter.

Finally, we need our new member programs to stop being the be-all, end-all. Education and development should continue throughout your whole undergraduate membership— perhaps even after graduation. Membership shouldn't be a goal with an end in sight; it should be a continuous process. Maybe that's the mentality that will help us move fraternity forward.

Joseph Thompson is a student affairs professional with 8+ years of experience focusing on furthering the fraternity/ sorority movement, facilitating student leadership and personal development, and advocating social justice issues. He is the Assistant Director of Student Development at Stockton University.

Joseph has a Master's Degree in College Student Affairs from Rutgers University, and a Bachelor's Degree in History and Secondary Education from Susquehanna University. Joseph is a brother of Phi Mu Delta Fraternity and is currently serving as the National Treasurer.

You can see Joseph's programs at www.greekuniversity.org/ joseph

Email Joseph: joseph@greekuniversity.org

CHAPTER 3

Peer Education and Intervention:
A Viable Tool to Prevent Hazing

Dr. Jason Meriwether

Hazing within fraternities and sororities has remained prevalent, alarming, and seemingly without end. Recent cases demonstrated the perpetual nature of hazing violence. In January of 2020, the Kappa Sigma Fraternity chapter at New Mexico State University was suspended for five years after the accidental shooting of pledge Jonathan Sillas. Chapter member Miguel Altamirano was shot during a November 2019 hazing ritual where pledges took a chapter-centric loyalty oath to the fraternity.[18]

---

[18]   Algernon D'Ammassa, "NMSU bans Kappa Sigma fraternity for 5 years after student was shot in hazing incident," *Las Cruces Sun-News*, January 23, 2020, https://www.lcsun-news.com/story/news/education/

Bowling Green State University sophomore Stone Foltz was killed during a hazing ritual involving alcohol consumption at an off-campus location while joining the Pi Kappa Alpha fraternity. Following the indictment of eight fraternity members, the first student, Niall Sweeney, 21, plead guilty of felony tampering with evidence and misdemeanor hazing. Sweeney and his seven co-defendants were also charged with involuntary manslaughter, hazing, obstruction, and failure to comply with underage alcohol laws.[19]

UC Riverside student, Tyler Hillard, was twenty years old when he died the day after hiking Mt. Rubidoux and participating in a "golden paddle night" as part of illegal hazing rituals while joining Alpha Phi Alpha Fraternity, Inc. in September of 2018. Hillard's parents Myeasha Kimble and William Hilliard have filed a wrongful death suit Superior Court in Riverside.[20]

Virginia Commonwealth University freshman Adam Oaks died the day after a fraternity rush event involving alcohol, according to the student's cousin, Courtney White. While attempting to join VCU's chapter of Delta Chi fraternity, Oakes died at an off-campus residence following a night of

nmsu/2020/01/23/new-mexico-state-university-bans-fraternity-kappa-sigma-hazing-shooting/4546570002/.

[19] Sheridan Hendrix, "First Bowling Green student pleads guilty in hazing death of Stone Foltz," *The Columbus Dispatch*, September 16, 2021, https://www.dispatch.com/story/news/education/2021/09/16/stone-foltz-first-bowling-green-student-pleads-guilty-hazing-death/8364449002/.

[20] Fisher Jack, "Parents of Tyler Hilliard File Lawsuit Against Alpha Phi Alpha Fraternity for Death by Hazing," *Apple News*, December 20, 2019, https://eurweb.com/2019/12/20/parents-of-tyler-hilliard-file-lawsuit-against-alpha-phi-alpha-fraternity-for-death-by-hazing-presser-announced/.

hazing and excessive alcohol consumption. Following Mr. Oaks's death in February of 2021, eleven VCU students were arrested as a result of an investigation. All of the arrested students were charged with unlawful hazing. Additional charges of buying and providing alcohol to a minor were filed against six of the offenders.

Jordan Hankins, a student athlete at Northwestern University committed suicide in January of 2017 following hazing and brutality perpetrated by members of the local chapter of Alpha Kappa Alpha Sorority during the fall of 2016. Ms. Hankins's family filed a federal lawsuit in January of 2019 in US District Court in Illinois. The lawsuit cites violent and tormenting hazing practices that "negatively affected [Ms. Hankins's] physical, mental, and emotional health." The lawsuit outlines "physical abuse including paddling, verbal abuse, mental abuse, financial exploitation, sleep deprivation, items being thrown and dumped on her, and other forms of hazing intended to humiliate and demean her."[21]

In 2017, Timothy Piazza, died following an alcohol field hazing ritual while pledging the Beta Theta Pi Fraternity chapter at Penn State University. After two falls during a night of heavy drinking, the chapter members of Beta Theta Pi failed to seek medical care for Mr. Piazza until the next day. In the following years, criminal investigations have resulted in jail time and civil action against multiple members of the local chapter.[22]

---

[21] Dakin Andone, "Sorority hazing led to Northwestern student's suicide, lawsuit claims," CNN, January 11, 2019, https://www.cnn.com/2019/01/10/us/jordan-hankins-northwestern-aka-sorority-lawsuit/index.html.

[22] John Beauge, "Settlements reached with 25 of 42 defendants in suit over 2017 Piazza hazing death at Penn State," *PennLive*, March 30, 2021, https://

Jeffrey Hall stated, "In light of annual instances of student injury as a result of risk-related behaviors on college and university campuses, programs and policies should be implemented to mitigate liability and minimize risky behaviors."[23] In spite of the call for greater engagement by university and campus leaders to preventatively combat hazing, student exposure to meaningful educative measures to prevent hazing is limited. Only 15% of students report being exposed to hazing prevention workshops conducted by adults, while only 14% report having been engaged through peer-led anti-hazing education workshops.[24] Gregory Parks noted, "Promoting the establishment of a more informed student body could reduce the likelihood that pledges will actively seek a hazing experience."[25] Simple policy dissemination or one-time presentations are inadequate levers to engage the topic of hazing. Others have noted, "There is a huge difference between setting up a system that can withstand a legal challenge and actually pursuing a course of action that will deal with the core problem."[26] Succinctly, to combat this

www.pennlive.com/news/2021/03/settlements-reached-with-25-of-42-defendants-in-suit-over-2017-piazza-hazing-death-at-penn-state.html.

[23] Jeffery D. Hall, "Risk Reduction and Fraternal Organizations: Tort Liability, Legislation, and Suggestions for Practice," *The Research Journal of the Association of Fraternity/Sorority Advisors*, September 2009, p. 30.

[24] Elizabeth Allan and Mary Madden, "Hazing in View: College Students at Risk," March 11, 2008, https://stophazing.org/wp-content/uploads/2020/12/hazing_in_view_study.pdf.

[25] Gregory Scott Parks, "Changing Hazing Attitudes (and Hopefully Behavior) Among Black 'Greeks,'" Wake Forest University Legal Studies Paper, No. 2184497, December 4, 2012, p. 37, http://ssrn.com/abstract=2184497.

[26] Howard E. Bailey and Aaron W. Hughey, "A Realistic, Pro-Active Approach to Eradicating Hazing for Greek Organizations," *Diverse: Issues in Higher Education*, January 16, 2013, http://diverseeducation.com/article/50714/.

problem, colleges and universities need to address hazing in legal, social, and educational contexts.

Involvement in Greek Letter Organizations

Student involvement is a critical element of the college student experience and exists as a key factor in student engagement and sense of belonging. It is also important for universities to provide quality opportunities for students to connect to the campus. Terrell Strayhorn described four ways student involvement increases connectedness and sense of belonging while in college:

1. connecting students with others who share their interests, values, and commitments;
2. familiarizing students with the campus environment and ecology;
3. affirming students' identity, interests, and values as "a part of campus" . . . and
4. generating feelings among students that they matter and others depend on them.[27]

As undergraduate students seek to mitigate challenges, establish greater engagement, and increase connectedness to their institution, one of the opportunities to meet these needs comes through Fraternity and Sorority Life. Joining a fraternity or sorority can help students combat feelings of

---

[27] Terrell Lamont Strayhorn, *College Students' Sense of Belonging: A Key to Educational Success for All Students* (Oxfordshire, England: Routledge, 2012), 115.

loneliness, develop social networks on campus, establish new friendships, and increase feelings of acceptance within the campus community. Describing the appeal of fraternities and sororities to new students, Hank Nuwer explained,

> Social organizations become even more attractive if they are perceived as providing entrance into a campus group with prestige, a way of meeting attractive members of the opposite sex, an opportunity to belong to a group that values participation in sports or other activities, or something meaningful that can be put on a resume.[28]

A positive relationship has been seen between fraternity and sorority membership and self-esteem, intellectual gains, and increased feelings of security and connection on campus. Martin, Hevel, and Pascarella shared the perspective of campus and national organization advisors, who express, "Their organizations attract leaders, provide leadership opportunities, improve leadership skills, and provide advantages in assuming prominent leadership positions on campus."[29] Consistently, Shawn Peoples in his doctoral dissertation postulated:

> Fraternities and sororities play an integral role in the social life of many college students. Being a part of a Greek-letter organization provides a sense of

---

[28] Hank Nuwer, *Wrongs of Passage: Fraternities, Sororities, Hazing, and Binge Drinking* (Bloomington, IN: Indiana University Press, 2001), 39.

[29] Georgianna L. Martin, Michael S. Hevel, and Ernest Pascarella, "Do Fraternities and Sororities Still Enhance Socially Responsible Leadership? Evidence from the Fourth Year of College," *Journal of Student Affairs Research and Practice* 49(3): 267.

brotherhood or sisterhood that will remain with a person for the rest of his or her life. It also provides a means for students to be involved in public service activities through which they will be able to give back to their community.[30]

Where It Went Wrong?

Nuwer posited that hazing is used to create a system in which current members are dominant over new initiates by perpetuating abusive practices to prove their worth. He explained that the hazing perpetrators are positioned to establish the terms of fraternal membership. Ricky Jones explained, "Specific hazing tactics are nothing more than creative variations deployed by individual fraternity members to push initiates to their limits in a supposed effort to establish their worthiness."[31] Jones described this process as forcing an initiate to prove their worth as well as their manliness because of the literal application of torture during the fraternal initiation process.

Caroline Keating and others extensively discussed hazing practices and initiation rituals among undergraduate students in GLOs and among student athletes. They explained that "initiations provide early opportunities for group leaders to establish power over newcomers to the organization"

---

[30] Shawn D. Peoples, "Tragedy or Tradition: The Prevalence of Hazing in African American Fraternities and Sororities" (2011 Doctoral Dissertation), p. 16, Retrieved from ProQuest Dissertations & Theses Global (3465498).

[31] Ricky L. Jones, *Black Haze: Violence, Sacrifice, and Manhood in Black Greek-Letter Fraternities Second Edition* (Albany: State University of New York, 2004), 63.

and were defined as inclusive of "activities perceived to be fun and rewarding, physically and emotionally demanding, embarrassing, socially deviant, degrading, painful, and sometimes dangerous or brutal."[32] Initiation rituals include adherence to very prescriptive traditions within the group that may include clearly assigned and defined roles for established members, to the end of repeating experiences of current members. In these instances the initiation process is rationalized by the concept that initiates are on a path to being better and more productive members of the group. Keating et al. delineated the aims of certain types of rituals in detail, noting,

> Certain types of initiation activities seem orchestrated to achieve particular effects. Experiencing physical extremes may train initiates to withstand physical duress. Engaging in social deviance may primarily function to etch distinction between the in-group and normative groups in the minds and emotions of initiates. Maltreatment may elicit cognitive, behavioral, and emotional symptoms of social dependency. From a functional perspective, different types of initiation experiences seem designed to preserve group features and cultivate group allegiance in particular ways.[33]

Allan and Madden noted that in "95% of the cases where students identified their experience as hazing, 'they did

---

[32] Caroline F. Keating, Jason Pomerantz, Stacy D. Pommer et al., "Going to College and Unpacking Hazing," *Group Dynamics: Theory, Research, and Practice* 9(2): 107, 105.

[33] Ibid., 106.

not report the events to campus officials'" and encouraged training students to "recognize the potential for harm even in activities they consider to be 'low level.'"[34] Consistent with this study, "A common perception among students is that the hazing ritual promotes group unity."[35] Dr. Walter Kimbrough discussed the willingness to submit to hazing rituals, without respect to illegality or safety, in order to satisfy a desire to belong.[36]

While one theory cannot substantively capture the full scope of the broad and pervasive nature of hazing, nor can it fully rationalize decisions to report hazing violence, a number of theories have been applied to conduct research in order to understand and ultimately mitigate the violence.

| *Social Norms Theory*

Regarding the impact of social norms, research on drinking, violence, and creating sense of responsibility among men explained men's behavior is determined by how they perceive that their counterparts perceive a situation, even if rooted in an incorrect perception. Alan David Berkowitz described the unintended consequences of such misperceptions among men, including tacit approval, passive observation, and failure to intervene or voice disapproval to negative behavior in dangerous or problematic situations. Berkowitz postulated,

---

[34] Allan and Madden, "Hazing in View," (2008), 2, 39.

[35] M. Gilroy, "Guns, hazing, and cyberbullying among top legal issues on college campuses," *The Education Digest* 78(8), 45–50.

[36] Walter Kimbrough, "Black Greek Deathwatch," Diverse Issues in Higher Education 26: 21.

Violence prevention is facilitated when individuals can identify situations with the potential for violence and then act to prevent it. Whether someone intervenes is in turn influenced by the extent to which they feel that others in their immediate environment share their concerns and will support their efforts.[37]

Social Dependency and Social Deviance

Keating et al. examined the impact of social dependency, physicality, social deviance, embarrassment, and conveyance of hierarchical standards within the context of initiation rituals. In their study, they measured participant attitudes toward their own initiation rituals, capturing their perceptions of the degree of power established by group leaders and assessing their perception of rituals as fun, embarrassing, physically and psychologically challenging, socially deviant or abnormal, and painful. Athletic group members demonstrated greater significant experiences of pain and physicality than did fraternity and sorority members, while fraternity and sorority members reported more embarrassment and social deviancy than study participants in athletic groups. Among participants, initiation rituals perceived as fun demonstrated significant influence on group importance among individual members, as did harsh initiations, which led to elevated perception of group importance by initiates. While more prevalent in fraternities and sororities, as noted above, social

---

[37] Alan David Berkowitz, "Fostering healthy norms to prevent violence and abuse: The social norms approach" in K. L. Kaufman's *The Prevention of Sexual Violence: A Practitioner's Sourcebook* (Holyoke, MA: NEARI Press, 2010), 3.

deviance did not correlate significantly with the value of group importance and identity.[38]

Groupthink and Greek Leadership Organizations

Groupthink is a process of group decision-making that reaches extremity of seeking consensus and undermines effectiveness of a group or organization. Groupthink can occur in any environment where decision-making is the responsibility of a group. Irving Janis explained groupthink, noting "concurrence seeking becomes so dominant in a cohesive ingroup [sic] that it tends to override realistic appraisal of alternative course of action."[39]

Applying the concept of groupthink within the context of hazing, Nuwer posited the term "Greekthink" as an adaptation of groupthink theory. Delineating the concept of Greekthink, Nuwer said that it can be viewed

> as a way of explaining what happens in fraternal groups that engage in negligent and dangerous behaviors during hazing, act as if members and pledges were invincible, value group practices above individual human rights, and deny that there is anything wrong with the uncivil rites they take part in.[40]

---

[38] Keating et al., "Going to college and unpacking hazing."
[39] Irving L. Janis, *Victims of Groupthink: A Psychological Study of Policy Decisions and Fiascos* (Boston: Houghton Mifflin, 1972), 45.
[40] Nuwer, *Wrongs of Passage*, 51.

| *Need for Esteem*

Morris Rosenberg described self-esteem as a favorable or unfavorable attitude toward the self, succinctly stated as, "a positive or negative attitude toward a particular object, namely, the self."[41] Rosenberg's definition of self-esteem has been considered the most revered and frequently cited among scholars. Self-esteem captures the cognitive and behavioral aspects of an individual's sense of self-worth and value and self-approval and appreciation. Describing self-esteem as a measure of personal worth, Rosenberg stated,

> High self-esteem, as reflected in our scale items, expresses the feeling that one is "good enough." The individual simply feels that he is a person of worth . . . Low self-esteem, on the other hand, implies self-rejection, self-dissatisfaction, and self-contempt. The individual lacks respect for the self he observes. The picture is disagreeable, and he wishes it were otherwise.[42]

Within the context of hazing, self-esteem can be present as a factor influencing the victim to voluntarily submit, the perpetrator to victimize, and the intent to report violent hazing behaviors. In detail,

> Self-esteem is bolstered by a sense of accomplishment and acceptance by others. "Surviving" hazing may contribute to a sense of achievement and garner

---

[41] Morris Rosenberg, *Society and the Adolescent Self-Image* (Princeton, NJ: Princeton University Press, 1965), 30.
[42] Ibid., 31.

the "respect" of group members, both of which can enhance individuals' esteem. Those who haze may enhance their own sense of esteem and heroism by maintaining membership in a group that "weeds out the weak."[43]

Range of Concepts

Elon University offered a myriad of theoretical concepts that may be factors in the decision to become complicit in, perpetuate, or fail to report acts associated with hazing violence. This range of explanations include the following:

- **Evolutionary psychology:** Our ancestors survived by forming groups that had strong bonds. Consequently, we are social creatures with needs for affiliation. Our innate drives for connection and preservation may contribute to practices such as hazing that are perceived to strengthen the ties between group members.
- **Lack of external constraints:** The social order of civilizations depends on accountability and shared agreement to conform to behavioral norms. When external security is decreased (e.g., in the aftermath of natural disasters), conformity to societal standards decreases (e.g., looting). In the absence of strong internal leadership and prosocial norms, groups that operate in secrecy, isolated from external constraints, are at greater risk of deviating

---

[43] Elon University, "Why do groups haze members?" Theories and Research, Theory, (n.d.), https://www.elon.edu/u/hazing/facts/theories-research/.

from societal norms of conduct. Hazing among students, the abuse of prisoners in Iraq, and the Enron corporate scandal each reflect in part the absence of external constraints on group behavior.

• **Sociopathy**: Some individuals within groups have personalities characterized by anti-social tendencies. Psychologically speaking, "anti-social" does not mean "doesn't like to party." Rather, it means traits such as disregard for the rights and safety of others, failure to conform to societal norms, and lack of remorse. While such individuals tend to be a small subset of groups, they can exert significant influence as hazing ringleaders.

• **Identification with the aggressor**: Intensive hazing can involve complex strategies to "break down" individuals and "remold" them to conform to the belief structures of the group. The group may isolate new members and expose them to repeated experiences designed to conform the new member's beliefs to those of the group. They may be told that the group is special and superior and that attainment of this status is worth whatever must be endured to achieve it. Eventually, new members may desire to become like the individuals who abuse them.

• **Shared coping**: When individuals go through a highly stressful experience together (e.g., a natural disaster, a battle), they may feel closer to each other as a result. Enduring hazing together may make a group feel more unity, but as with hurricanes, the experience may yield damage as well as benefits.

- **Cycles of abuse:** Individuals who are hazed may be at greater risk of hazing others because of a displaced desire for revenge. As one fraternity pledge said immediately after being hazed intensely, "I can't wait to do this to the pledges next year." In addition, being hazed involves a learning process by which members model for new members the accepted methods for initiation.

- **Perceived lack of alternatives:** While the underlying needs of individuals and groups can be met through non-hazing means, a lack of knowledge about those means and an absence of creativity enables individuals to perpetuate the belief that hazing is necessary. When presented with credible alternatives, many individuals agree to pursue them in place of hazing.

- **Misperceived norms:** In some groups, the majority of members believe that it is not important to humiliate, intimidate, or physically abuse new members. These members, however, mistakenly believe that they are in the minority. They may therefore reluctantly perpetuate these practices because they assume that everyone else believes that they are the right things to do.[44]

While each of the concepts above fits within certain contexts of hazing culture, they also demonstrate the range and breadth of entry points for hazing to erode and corrode the value system, norms, and culture of Greek Letter Organizations. Due to the overwhelming range of violence,

---

[44] Ibid.

risks, dangers, and hidden harms, it has become evident that campus leaders must explore all available strategy levers to reduce and mitigate the effects of hazing. In particular, campus leaders should leverage Peer Intervention as a lever to mitigate hazing.

Recommendations for Effective Practice

Peer Intervention and Education

Berkowitz adapted social norms theory as a comprehensive strategy and tool to combat and mitigate sexual violence within fraternal culture and systems and to explore. In my book, *Dismantling Hazing in Greek-Letter Organizations*, I suggest adapting and leveraging social norms theory to generate healthy conversations within fraternal systems to review, discuss, and generate discussion about drinking and violence.

> As universities enact policy levers and educative programs to encourage students to report hazing behavior, it is important to recognize how underrepresented populations cope with feelings of connectedness to the campus in general and how these feelings may be exacerbated within the social structure of a sorority or fraternity.[45]

Berkowitz encourages the facilitation of peer engagement and intervention as significant violence prevention levers through teaching training individuals to identify and speak

---

[45] Jason L. Meriwether, *Dismantling Hazing in Greek-Letter Organizations: Effective Practices for Prevention, Response, and Campus Engagement* (Washington, DC: NASPA, 2020), 248.

against potential violence or harm in hazing situations. Within the context of fraternal culture, there are often false assumptions that other chapter members do not object to violent hazing behavior and remain silent due to tacit or outright approval of the violence.

I encourage campus leaders to organize and sustain peer-engagement sessions for fraternity and sorority members, aspiring members, and non-members. It would be effective to conduct "situational training on how to respond and report hazing when it is observed. Creating a student-led council that is tasked to combat hazing through supporting peer-intervention measures can also strengthen peer intervention."[46]

To implement and sustain an effective model for peer and behavioral intervention, I offer a model for leaders on campus and across the FSL community. The Meriwether Peer Intervention & Prevention model provides a series of levers to create, sustain, and assess peer intervention strategies. Each phase of the model includes five levers. The first phase compels campus and FSL leaders to Cultivate a System of Commitment. Commitment to hazing prevention includes structures for support, dedicated resources, systems of group accountability, stable support structures, clear policies, and active participation of senior leadership. The cultivation phase includes the following five levers:

1. *Demonstrate Commitment of Senior Leaders.* It is important for senior campus leaders to partner with FSL professionals throughout

---

[46] Ibid.

this process, to remain physically present, and to commit resources to peer intervention as a hazing prevention strategy lever. The support system must empower FSL professionals to and remain consistent before there is a hazing issue. I published a paper with Elizabeth Allen where we describe the participation of senior leadership as "vital," noting that such commitment "should include public messaging about expectations for inclusive, welcoming, and safe group behavior rather than potentially threating, humiliating, or abusive behavior."[47]

2. *Establish Stakeholder Partnerships.* Allan et al. elevate the value of a robust coalition of stakeholders on and off campus, noting the efficacy of participation "across institutional divisions (e.g., athletics, fraternity/sorority life, student activities, health and wellness, student leadership, student conduct) and stakeholder groups (e.g., students, faculty, staff, parents, and alumni)."[48] It is necessary for such broad engagement in order to provide consistent messaging and support for peer intervention. These engagements should not be singular in nature and should not occur only in the begin-

---

[47] Elizabeth J. Allan and Jason L. Meriwether, "Preventing Campus Hazing: VPSAs Can Help Lead the Institutional Commitment to Change," Fall 2019, *Leadership Exchange* 17(3): 17; https://www.leadershipexchange-digital.com/lexmail/2019fall/MobilePagedReplica.action?utm_source=newsletter&utm_medium=email&utm_campaign=TXLEAD191007002&pm=2&folio=10#pg12.

[48] Elizabeth J. Allan, Jessica M. Payne, and David Kerschner, "Transforming the Culture of Hazing," *Journal of Student Affairs Research and Practice* 55(4): 412–425. DOI: 10.1080/19496591.2018.1474759.

ning of the strategy lever. Consistency in participation from stakeholders on and off campus will
strengthen the efficacy of peer intervention efforts.

3. *Clarify Reporting Structures.* As an aspect of Peer
    Intervention, it is important to have consistent
    and public messaging about reporting options
    and resources. I encourage the facilitation of
    "open-campus and small-group sessions during
    orientation or welcome weeks to discuss hazing
    in GLOs. Sessions should include students and
    parents and facilitate direct conversation about
    the risks of hazing."[49] Such sessions should also
    include sharing hazing prevention resources and
    reporting tools across the campus community for
    those receiving reports, or others making reports.
    In particular, clarifying reporting structures for
    aspiring, new, and current members can aid in
    sustaining the peer intervention model.

4. *Facilitate Training and Certification.* I introduced a
    hazing prevention education model that suggests
    a "student-led initiative that provides situational
    training on how to respond and report when
    hazing is observed."[50] Social norms theory offers
    a framework for corrective intervention strategies
    to mitigate misperceptions by revealing that most
    individuals in a setting prefer the healthier and safer
    option, yielding a beneficial effect on the group
    and yielding a lower likelihood of participating
    in violent or problematic behaviors. Training

---

[49] Meriwether, *Dismantling Hazing in Greek-Letter Organizations*, 75.
[50] Ibid., 249.

should include direct conversations and explore the feelings, perceptions, and misconceptions about hazing and violence. Campus leaders should create training spaces where students may "openly share their perspectives about hazing in a group setting, with specific discussions that focus on how risks of danger and harm outweigh the perceived consequences of failing to report hazing."[51] The investment of time, capacity, and funds to facilitate peer intervention training for students, advisors, alumni, organizational leaders, and other campus stakeholders is necessary. This lever provides the foundational tools and strategies to engage and challenge violent and problematic behavior through demonstrations, role-playing, and facilitating earnest discussion between organization members.

5. *Implement FSL Council and Peer Intervention Model.* This council is a public-facing group of GLO members tasked to combat hazing by supporting peer-intervention measures and publicly and privately oppose hazing. Such a council is critical to peer intervention efforts, in particular if it is driven by a group of engaged students that are trained, involved in policy discussions, planning, and execution of peer-intervention as a key hazing prevention lever. This council must receive ongoing attention and communication with university leaders, and receive support from FSL professionals and beyond. Optimally, such a council would receive a budget that is additive

---

[51] Ibid.

to existing FSL funding. Website presence, marketing support, and consistent in the planning and development of the training and certification described in lever four (above) would assist with the efficacy of peer intervention strategies. This group should also be consistently engaged in the assessment efforts described in Phase Two.

The Phase Two strategy to Sustain a System of Commitment includes the following five strategy levers:

1. *Sustain FSL Council and Peer Intervention Model.* Campus leaders should focus on sustaining and empowering the student group and the model. Establishing an ongoing, cyclical, and calendared system of meetings, trainings, and engaging will help sustain momentum even with student turnover caused by changing leadership or natural cycles of change caused by graduation. Budget allocations must evolve annually to sustain continuity

2. *Ongoing Training and Recertification.* Peer Intervention training should remain an active part of the efforts to educate, aspiring, new, and current members as well as other campus stakeholders. Recertification should remain annual and be required for participation in new membership activities or certification to be an active student organization on campus.

3. *Sustained Marketing and Branding.* Budget allocation has been repeatedly discussed as part of this framework as a tool to enhance the efficacy of peer intervention as a strategy

lever. This investment must include funding a comprehensive marketing and branding campaign for Peer Intervention as a campus-wide initiative that does not only fall under the purview of FSL professionals. Catherine Allan and I also suggest "developing and widely distributing resources to all campus stakeholders that provide clear language to define hazing, explain the range of hazing behaviors and present strategies for determining when acceptable behavior crosses the line into hazing."[52] An effective branding and marketing investment includes campus and community messaging. This investment should be additive to existing FSL budgets.

4. *Expand Partnerships to Athletics and Campus Orgs.* Allan encourages a campus-wide approach to hazing prevention that is not limited to sororities and fraternities, noting that hazing reaches academic, athletics, on- and off-campus housing, and beyond. More than half of college students are hazed in the process of joining student organizations, which includes seven out of every ten students who join fraternities or sororities. Further, 47% of students come to college having experienced hazing.[53] These data present a compelling impetus to expand Peer Intervention efforts beyond the FSL community. Broadening the breadth and scope of peer intervention can position the FSL community to shift from the

---

[52] Allan and Meriwether, "Preventing Campus Hazing," (2019), 17.
[53] Allan and Madden, "Hazing in View" (2008).

historical position as purveyors of the hazing phenomena to an authentic position of leadership to eradicate hazing.

5. *Ongoing Assessment.* Catherine Allan and I suggest "allocating resources to regularly collect campus data about hazing and hazing prevention, including data on positive social norms."[54] StopHazing.org also offers a Campus Hazing Prevention Rubric as a tool to collect and curate data and self-assess progress toward hazing prevention goals. Further, Allan et al. delineate specific steps to consider when developing a system to assess hazing prevention data which include creating a system to track hazing incidents and associated sanctions; quantitative and qualitative surveys; environmental scans; and wide dissemination of collected data.[55] Without reservation, campus leaders should commit to a culture of assessing and measuring the efficacy of the strategy levers prescribed in this model. The continues and ongoing measurement and assessment of these efforts will provide a data-rich continuum in which to make decisions about growth, expansion, and future levers to increase the efficacious nature of peer intervention.

---

[54] Allan and Meriwether, "Preventing Campus Hazing," (2019), 17.

[55] Allan, Payne, and Kerschner, "Transforming the Culture of Hazing," (2018).

Figure 1 represents the Meriwether Peer Intervention & Prevention Model.

Figure 1.

Conclusion

The comprehensive and sustained investment and commitment to Peer Intervention as a tool to combat hazing must be campus-wide and include stakeholders on campus and beyond. Among the many choices that campus leaders are presented with to mitigate hazing, adopting a peer intervention model offers the potential to reach far beyond the traditional approaches and strategy levers.

Dr. Jason L. Meriwether is an experienced leader in higher education with research interests in hazing prevention, enrollment management, student retention, digital learning tools, adult student success, and social media engagement. In 2016, Jason was named to the Southern Indiana Business Source 20 under 40 Class of 2016. In 2014, Jason was selected to Louisville Business First's Top Forty under 40 and as one of Business First's 20 People to Know in Education and Workforce Development. In 2014, Jason received the award of Outstanding Kentuckian and was commissioned to the Honorable Order of Kentucky Colonels.

Jason is editor of *Dismantling Hazing in Greek-Letter Organizations: Effective Practices for Prevention, Response, and Campus Engagement.*

A native of Guthrie, Kentucky, Jason earned his Bachelor of Arts Degree in Communication from the University of Louisville. He earned the Master of Arts Degree in Psychology from Fisk University and earned the PhD in Educational Administration with a Specialization in Higher Education Leadership from Indiana State University.

Jason currently serves Humboldt State University as Vice President of Enrollment Management.

You can see Dr. Meriwether's presentations here: www.greekuniversity.org/jason

Email Jason: jason@greekuniversity.org

CHAPTER 4

"What, Like It's Hard?"

How Empathy and Authentic Relationships Lead to Active Bystander Intervention

Jamie Devin Wilson

I t was the fall of 2006. I had just gone through sorority recruitment. My experience was wonderful. I met members in all the houses that I could see being my lifelong friends. I heard there was one chapter that did not haze. As I got further along in the recruitment experience, I made my selections subconsciously because I just wasn't someone who wanted to be hazed. It seemed like the women were close in the chapter I was interested in, and that was something I wanted. We were told to sleep over on certain nights on the cold, alcohol-sticky basement floor. There was one mattress given to the fourteen of us. Our new member educator told us that we would just need to answer the older sister's questions and not be scared—that the organization does not haze.

We all stood there. It is silent and dark in the basement of the house. I can feel the heartbeats of the women I am holding hands with on either side of me. I barely know these women; we just met a few days ago. We are all in a circle facing outward. We are in order of our last names or initiation order. Older active sisters that I had not even met before stomped into the room. They stood in a line in front of the circle. Our eyes were to be closed. They asked us questions in intimidating voices. I remember hearing one of my new member sisters laughing a little and then getting yelled at. I thought it was ridiculous because the questions were things about the older sisters that we had no clue about.

This was hazing. Line-ups are hazing. They weren't our friends yet; we hardly knew these people. And those that might not want to participate or know it's inherently wrong do not yet have the tools to intervene through active bystander intervention—which is a crucial need to break the cycle of hazing and create change in organizations.

Additionally, members know it is hazing and just continue to do it because many want to. Many think it's the only way to form respect, belonging, and understanding. This is where organizations get it wrong. Hazing might bond people, but it doesn't develop an authentic connection and/ or brotherhood and sisterhood. It trauma-bonds people. Trauma bonding was defined by Cambridge University in

2020 as a connection between an abusive person and the individual they abuse. It typically occurs when the abused person begins to develop sympathy or affection for the abuser. In 2018 research from Cambridge investigating abuse in athletic organizations, the study suggests that Stockholm syndrome may start when a person experiencing abuse begins to rationalize the perpetrator's actions. It is a mentality that exists because we are simply too lazy to do the hard work it takes to form genuine, authentic, kind relationships. Relationships are work. But healthy relationships should be more critical to a group that prides itself on belonging that lasts a lifetime over trying to gain respect through trauma, fear, and intimidation.

Let's start creating programs rid of hazing, focusing on healthy relationships, and creating a culture that builds empathy and bystander intervention approaches. However, like Elle Woods from the movie *Legally Blonde*, we cannot think, *What, like it's hard?* This is because it IS hard. If it were easy to change the culture and social norms from over a hundred years of tradition, we wouldn't have the current issue of trying to help people understand the problems with perpetuating hazing culture. It is hard for three distinct reasons: 1) Sometimes criminal traditions have been passed down as normal and just something we all do. That mentality diminishes the harm and trauma that comes from the hazing. 2) As 18–22-year-olds, students' brains will not be fully formed physically yet, so the desire for belonging and excitement override the desire for safety and challenging the system. 3) It seems too hard to create change, and students rarely see the options or alternatives to hazing that work. We need to start moving the needle a lot quicker on hazing behavior, and we will only do that by integrating empathy in our new member education programs.

First off, if you simply google "alternatives to hazing," campuses, professionals, insurance companies, etc., have all written out ways to increase education and belonging without hazing. Hundreds of other options to hazing have been published in some form, so see the addendum for alternate new member activities. I will use this space to talk about developing real connections and how we can make that shift as changemakers.

Now, let's talk about empathy and authentic connection. Brené Brown states that connection is energy that exists when people feel seen, heard, and valued—when they give and receive without judgment and derive sustenance and strength from that relationship. If you do not build authentic connections as members of an organization, you do not have true brotherhood or sisterhood despite anything you want to believe. For centuries groups have been handing bids or other forms of invitations to a potential member and think immediately a bond is formed. What is created is an initial exchange of excitement, anxiety, nervousness, and the distinct desire to be a part of that group.

To form those authentic relationships and create belonging, organization members must resist the old hazing mentality. We need to make a shift; we need to understand empathy and use it in our educational processes and relationships to break the harmful programs and behaviors in organizations. Using and understanding empathetic exchanges to create authentic relationships is one answer to alternative forms to hazing.

Empathy comes in three forms, according to psychologists Daniel Goleman and Paul Ekman. Empathy feels different depending on how you give and receive it. It is essential to teach our active members practical empathy to build those relationships that lead to the goal of new member education—belonging. The three forms of empathy are *emotional, cognitive*, and *compassion*.

Emotional Definition: Perspective taking, understanding someone's perspective, or at least trying to.

What it's associated with: thought, understanding, intellect.

Benefits in practice: Helps in chapter/meeting settings, motivating members and understanding diverse ideas and viewpoints, and is ideal for virtual meetings and programs.

Pitfalls: This practice of empathy can feel disconnected—it doesn't put you in another's shoes in an authentic sense.

Cognitive Definition: "when you feel physically along with the other person, as though their emotions were contagious." —Daniel Goleman

What it's associated with: feelings amongst members' relationships, physical sensation during connection moments, members mirror neurons in the brain helping each person in that relationship genuinely feel what the other is feeling at a deep level.

Benefits in practice: Helps in close interpersonal relationships and relationships like big/little, vulnerability conversations with members, marketing for recruitment, management of chapter operations by understand members' feelings, and building authentic relationships.

Pitfalls: Can be overwhelming or inappropriate in certain circumstances. It is crucial members must create environments and spaces with psychological and physical safety before using emotional empathy.

Compassionate Definition: We not only understand someone's predicament, but we also holistically feel and harness their experience.

What it's associated with: intellect, emotion, and action.

Benefits in practice: Considers the whole member. Making sure kindness, conversation, clarity, and safety are all a part of this empathetic practice. Members can use this in meetings, discussions, activities, and pretty much whenever someone is looking to form a human connection.

Pitfalls: There are very little—this is the type of empathy that we're usually aiming for within organization member growth and development.

You can use these pathways to create authentic relationships where you would not want to hurt your friend. Whereas, if you barely have a relationship more than a bid agreement, you are more likely to harm someone, whether intentionally or not. If you genuinely care about someone's holistic well-being, you are more likely to intervene when something doesn't seem right, and you can get the right people on board to make changes.

Something that might disrupt unhealthy practices is to understand rites of passage and the perceived importance within Fraternity and Sorority Life. If our members focus less on initiation but more on the holistic education and relationship building throughout their lifetime membership, there may be less pressure to haze. I believe the antidote to hazing is authentic connection and love. You wouldn't haze someone you love. You wouldn't hurt someone you care about deeply. And the truth is you don't actually know someone in 6–8 weeks of new member education. Which means there needs to be a cultural shift of authentic connection building and belonging from forms of education and pressurized relationship bonding. This might mean the candidate learn the basics and subscribe to membership with initiation but then have intentional membership development processes through graduation and beyond. Putting an emphasis on learning, love, and connection throughout the member's lifetime commitment to their group. Shifting the mindset that upon initiation you are a *full* member, new members would need to uphold these virtues and values throughout their lifetime. As active members they would continually be educated, put in connection and vulnerable conversations, and intentionally need to live up to the chapter's values— not to earn letters, but to deepen their relationship with the organization's Ritual and virtues for a lifetime.

The impact of hazing in all forms causes stress, anxiety, pain, physical harm, emotional harm, and sometimes death. All forms of hazing are a crime, and mental and emotional hazing often leads to physical and more harmful activities as members feel the power of manipulation and hierarchy.

I want you to picture yourself at a recruitment event as an active member; potential new members are desperate to have genuine conversations. These conversations are hopefully on more than what they wore to the event. The potential new member asks you, "Does your organization haze?"

And just like your recruitment chair taught you, you politely look the person in front of you in the eye and say, "At (Organization) it is illegal to haze, and therefore we do not—also, would you think that I would ever put myself in a situation like that? I am a strong person, and strong people do not get hazed, that is so (insert year that you think is irrelevant)."

Would it not be extraordinary to not need to learn that elevator pitch? You answer because you can confidently say that all your members have empathetic and authentic relationships and practice active bystander intervention— that all your members care about each other.

To care about each other, members must learn forms of bystander intervention approaches. Often, the brains of an 18–22-year-old in trauma, whether they are receiving, doing, or a bystander, have a freeze response. This moment where the brain is giving you time to process flight or fight. In trauma and post-traumatic stress moments, humans tend to sit in the freeze longer than they might intend. This is your brain's natural response. Members should be taught how to become UNFROZEN which is an active bystander intervention approach. Let me process this acronym with you all and give some examples (this will not be exhaustive as there will be more examples than listed).

UNFROZEN™

U- *Under no circumstance, intervene unless you are safe to do so!*

> Example from hazing experience: Moments before, the older sisters walked into the basement, the New Member Educator could have told us to leave right now and that while the experience truly isn't harmful physically, that we really shouldn't need to go through this and that they would talk with the older members about better approaches for new member education.

N- Nonstop confrontation by being direct, clear, and concise

> Example from hazing experience: Any active member or new member trained in this theory and are feeling safe could be clear and direct and say they would not participate in this experience. Outline specifically why it does not create connection or belonging.

F- *Figure out a way to distract or de-escalate the situation*

> Example from hazing experience: When the new member laughed, diminishing the experience that the hazers set out to create—and other new members

and actives recognizing that this was unnecessary and cruel—active members could de-escalate the situation by turning on the lights. They could say they could do speed-dating to learn more about one another since the new members clearly did not know them well yet.

R- *Remember your resources and delegate them to a third party (911 or your campus hotline)*

Example from hazing experience: your advisors, headquarters, and staff at the University, along with crisis resources, are all there to assist. Following this event (or before to prevent), active sisters or new members could have called their Fraternity and Sorority Life advisor and worked with them to create an action plan to change the practices of this event and all events which are a part of the new member education process.

O- *Orient and organize yourself. Document and take notes on your phone of what you see and document details like addresses, names, etc.*

Z- *Zip up the situation by delaying and checking in with the participants while ending as quickly as possible*

Example from hazing experience: If you are an active member and uncomfortable with what is happening, you could check in with the participants and end the situation early, giving ample time to talk to leadership about a needed change.

E- *Engage with empathy*

> Example from hazing experience: All the members are bystanders during the hazing that know what was happening; the new members, however, are victims, so if you are going to intervene, engage with kindness, care, and careful attention to the situation.

N- *No matter what, believe the survivor*

> Example from hazing experience: If the member or new member shares that they think they were hazed, believe them. Period. Do not ask any questions; actively listen. Then move forward.

All in all, connection, friendship, and healthy relationships are not formed through trauma and hazing. They are formed holistically through empathy, vulnerability, and heart. They are created when we intervene in uncomfortable and harmful situations because we care about our members and not because we must. Hazing is a crime. Hazing should be treated as a crime. Think about your new member education process. Are your activities and events created to help new members learn about the organization and to create belonging? Are they focused on asking current and new members questions to better themselves to ultimately better the overall community? Are you taking the time before member education and utilizing resources to help your organization develop a plan, rid of hazing and full of empathy and compassion?

If you are ready to make that culture shift, I believe in you.

Case Study

Mya just received a bid from the sorority of her dreams. She was given the whole "we don't haze speech" at every house during Panhellenic recruitment. Although she sort of believed them, there were rumors that the organization that she just received a bid from watched a lot of hazing of other organizations. She knew she was uncomfortable with this situation. Still, since she wasn't being hazed or hazing, she just went along with it because she really wanted to be initiated and well-liked within her organization. She wanted to be a future leader and knew rocking the boat this early in her membership would not look good.

Mya found herself one night at a fraternity house with the rest of the new member class overlooking a courtyard. The fraternity president was with the sorority president and all the new members watching from windows. They both articulated that the new members could watch, but they needed to be quiet and never tell anyone. Mya immediately held the hand of one of her fellow new member friends and squeezed. She said, "I am not sure we should be watching." Another new member shushed Mya and said, "This is going to be hysterical. Just watch and shut up!" Mya's friend squeezed her hand, and the Fraternity president said, "You all can't leave now that you know about this. Don't worry, you all won't be a part of this, and you just need to stay put till it is over." Reiterating that the new members should not tell anyone. The sorority president just went along with the whole thing. From the window, Mya peered out and watched as the fraternity's new members were lined up in the courtyard. They were only wearing white underwear. They were all closing their eyes. The members of the Fraternity threw buckets of dirty water on them, peed on their shoes, threw bananas and mixtures of slop on them. When a new member of the Fraternity would laugh or say to stop, the Fraternity men started throwing more harmful items. Beer bottles, ladders, apples. Mya started to cry. She knew this was wrong. She thought to herself, *Doesn't everyone know this is wrong?* When the event was over, the fraternity president reiterated that this is their little secret. The sorority new members and president left the room.

1. What could have been done differently?
   a. Mya
   b. Presidents
   c. Organization

2. How could the chapter President have used the UNFROZEN™ intervention approach?
3. What would you have done if you were:
   a. Mya
   b. Chapter president
   c. New member

4. Look at your organization. Are they following a path to empathy, belonging, and connection? What have they done to make members' experiences better in this area? What have they not done?
5. What would you do?

Jamie is on a mission to end sexual violence, educate others in active bystander intervention, and uplift the Fraternity and Sorority Life experience. She cares deeply for the development and growth of not just college students but young professionals in the field of higher education.

She is a wife, sister, sorority woman, survivor of sexual violence, and student affairs professional in higher education. She enjoys coffee, yoga, REALLY long walks, and watching old episodes of *Gossip Girl* and *Greek*. Did we mention she is a sorority woman?!

Fraternity and sorority is woven through her blood, sweat, and tears. Jamie has been working with college students for over ten years in a variety of roles, including working for an inter/national sorority, on college campuses, and through facilitating and speaking.

Jamie graduated with a Bachelor's Degree in Journalism, and a minor in Leadership from the University of Rhode Island. After graduating she spent some time working in sales and for a social media marketing company. Shortly after, she worked for her inter/national organization in a variety of roles as a consultant, membership manager, and house director. After that Jamie went to Northeastern University for her Master's in College Student Development and Counseling and for the past three years she has been working at the University of New Hampshire overseeing the Fraternity and Sorority Life community there.

You can see Jamie's presentations here: www.greekuniversity. org/jamie

Email Jamie: jamie@greekuniversity.org

CHAPTER 5

Hidden Harms:
Exploring Risk and Dangers of Perceived Low-Level Hazing

Mel Lewis

"So . . . were you hazed?!" The first time someone asked me this question, I was in a perplexed state of shock. ME?! Mel Lewis . . . HAZED?! *Insert Italian hand emoji here*

I would be lying if I said I never associated Fraternity and Sorority Life with hazing; heck, I am pretty sure everyone has at one point. The reality is that prior to entering a higher educational institute, we are only exposed to perceptions: movies, TV, the news, social media, personal stories, etc. Just as there is a lack of education on consent in secondary education, there is a similar approach to hazing. Simply saying "don't haze" is not going to banish it entirely. The true disservice is avoiding discussions around effective communication and creating a sense of individual values at an early age.

When I entered college, I was uninformed regarding the world of fraternity and sorority. I did not see the purpose of "paying for my friends" since I already had a flourishing social life as a college freshman. I would roll my eyes at the stories of what people "had to do" in order to become a member of one of these organizations. I, however, never imagined a situation where I myself would be questioned about being hazed; not only did I ever think I would be affiliated with Fraternity and Sorority Life, but I also knew that I was not someone who would haze or be hazed.

What's important to note was that I was a founding member of my chapter on my campus where we were able to establish the bylaws and structure of our membership. There were not any "traditions" yet because we hadn't created or established them. Our International Headquarters staff and volunteers that aided our education were outstanding and patient, considering they were working with ninety women at a small college in New Jersey. I'd be lying to you if I said we didn't meet in private to discuss socials with alcohol (not sure if they are called mixers anymore), since that was not something we were readily allowed to do. I remember the evening that someone brought up hazing like it was yesterday. "Should we haze our new members when we eventually get them?" The room was a mixture of awkward silence, tensions, and sound effects of shock that are normal for college students. No one wanted to be the first to speak, yet we were all yearning to have the conversation. The member who posed the question looked around, shrugged her shoulders, and exclaimed "Everyone else has their new members prove themselves . . . why can't we?"

This thought process confused me at the time (and to be honest, still does a bit). In my opinion, we did prove ourselves based on our values, our passion, and our commitment to not only learning about our organization, but the world of fraternity and sorority. Being qualified for the position of membership is established in the recruitment process (and if you disagree, then enhance your recruitment strategies). Amongst all the chatter and heated conversations, a member finally made a statement that allowed us to move forward: "We don't have to prove ourselves to the other chapters on campus and vice versa; why would we ask anyone to do something that we ourselves would never do?" The room filled with stern snaps, and we made it a mission of ours to not compare roses amongst other flowers.

I believe this was the moment I became bewildered at the idea of hazing and where it exists in Fraternity and Sorority Life. I reached further into my fascination when I became Panhellenic president the following semester and was able to read the entire manual, which states the premise of what is allowed and not allowed. One of the things I found was the whole myth behind how Panhellenic members cannot wear stitched letters prior to being initiated is in fact hazing. When I exclaimed this to others, they simply answered, "That type of hazing isn't that big of a deal."

One thing to know about me is I am a rule follower. No, I am not perfect, and I most certainly have had some missteps, but I always look for the why behind rules and am not one to disregard them. All types of hazing are a big deal. The reason I stand very firmly on this point is that we welcome all types of members into our organizations. These members all come from diverse experiences and different understandings of who they are. Just as there is no exact way of knowing how the fraternal experience will impact members, there is no way of knowing how hazing will impact them as people.

Now, you might be flipping back the pages and thinking "Mel, I thought this was a chapter on low-risk hazing? I thought there were types of hazing that are not that big of a deal!" Yes, reader, you are correct in how I am here today to expand upon how hazing is classified into two different risk levels: high risk and low risk. Let's view the two different levels and some examples in order to get a better understanding of what we will be focusing on in this chapter.

High-Risk Hazing: acts of violence, involving substances such as alcohol and drugs, sleep deprivation, and performing degrading and dangerous tasks

Low-Risk Hazing: wearing uniforms, mandating or prohibiting, specific names, embarrassing tasks and behaviors

High-risk hazing, which is usually depicted in movies and is unfortunately a reality for most campuses, usually stems from a culture created by the chapter, the campus, or the types of members who have joined in the past. It is, unfortunately, difficult to unlearn these actions and mindsets and are what keep most fraternity and sorority professionals up at night trying to think of its cure. When it comes to low-risk hazing, it can happen to any chapter or organization if they are not more aware of their culture internally and externally.

Just to be clear, each state, institution, and organization has varying definitions of how certain rules are defined, causing there to be loopholes or a vague understanding of the why overall. Based on my experience as a Student Affairs professional, working and volunteering with Greek members, these low-risk hazing examples are some of the most common and most talked about unknowingly in advisement meetings I have had. Since these types of hazing are rarely warned about or discussed openly, I want to take the time to explain a bit further.

Uniforms: can be considered anything that is being mandated to wear. This isn't the simple "wear black to a funeral" concept but more "you wear this to distinguish yourself as a new member." Are there certain old school tips that I would stand behind today that I learned from my own organization, absolutely. As a thirty-year-old, I still won't have a glass of wine with dinner if I am wearing my stitched letters because you never drink in your letters. Sure, there a few outdated ones, but at the end of the day, new members should be able to express themselves and feel comfortable while entering the world of fraternity and sorority.

Prohibiting new members to attend meetings but then trying to mandate them later: Yes, I already know what you're thinking: *Mel . . . new members cannot attend these meetings if we hold Ritual or are doing any voting.* I understand that completely . . . but do they? Does your chapter take the time to explain the function of meetings and why certain ones are done under Ritual or are we just making it look as if we are doing something that is above their worthiness? A simple fix: have the meeting be open once Ritual is conducted; explain to them that meetings serve a purpose, and they are not something "you have to do."

Anyone reading this has probably also heard a new member claim they were being hazed because they "were mandated" to attend a meeting. While this is frustrating, take a deep breath. When a person agrees to accept an invitation of membership, they are agreeing to attend what is necessary for them to learn the education and culture of the chapter and organization. If your chapter is not laying out these expectations, then make sure to do so either during recruitment or at the start of the new member process. Always make sure the new member process is outlined with outcomes and clear time commitments (think how your professors provide you a syllabus for each class). Remember to not assume that they know what to expect; have a non-affiliated friend or roommate read over it before presenting it. (Relax, your New Member Education Plan for your organization is public knowledge. Your New Member Education Plan for your specific chapter should also be public knowledge.)

Specific names: if you know me, you know that if I am in the presence of students who use the term "baby" or "pledge" regarding new members, it physically pains me. Yes, there are certain people who will say it in a joking way, sure. But understanding the message that it projects is important to comprehend: these new members are most likely younger than you, but they are not beneath you. They are not cute or pathetic—they are new to the world of Greek Life and are no lesser than yourself or other older members. Specific names or phrases that are consistently associated with a new member class or that they might be expected to address the rest of the chapter by could create a stigma and, once again, has no purpose to them becoming exceptional members.

Greek organizations are always getting involved with their campus community, but there are some aspects that might make members uncomfortable that should be considered:

Getting to know every member of the chapter: this is not a requirement of membership; this is a way for chapters to create a forced sense or brotherhood/sisterhood/siblingship. True connections are created organically, but a simple fix could be to have organized opportunities for members to learn about each other. An activity or event where the members are grouped by birth month could be a way to have casual yet meaningful conversations with a variety of members instead of awkward interview-like set-ups. Who needs to know every member's major or hometown in order to really feel connected to them, am I right?

Group activities: Are there some great free workout classes or concerts on college campuses that you might want to engage in as a chapter, especially with new members? OF COURSE! Mandating them, however, can be a bit tricky with comfort levels and boundaries. I once was facilitating a conversation around new member activities with a fraternity, and they mentioned how they have mandated gym hours. Their justification was that one of their organization's values was wellness, and they believed their new members should embody that value. I applaud the involvement of a chapter's values in New Member Education, but I clearly have to point out the obvious here. Unlike mandating study or educational hours to improve grades or knowledge, all members define the values of their organization differently (that's the whole point!). To mandate members to define wellness, for example, as going to the gym for a certain amount of time per week is a bit like forcing them to believe in one set example of wellness.

Just as there are different levels of hazing, I would view low-risk hazing as having three different sections as well:

1. All for One: the idea that if everyone participates, it will make them stronger as a group or that if everyone participates, it won't be as bad.
2. Groupthink: the idea that it is what it is, and it is normal because the chapter said it was.
3. Isolation: the idea that if someone does not participate, they care less or are not taking it seriously. It could also refer to the idea of FOMO (fear of missing out) and be thrown into someone's face later.

Low-risk hazing may invalidate the feeling of individualism with members and their viewpoints; it creates a space of exclusion, resentment, and disengagement. You took the first steps here and learned more thoroughly about the different levels and types of hazing (give yourself a pat on the back, this topic is never easy). Let's talk about the next steps if you notice this type of behavior exists in your chapter or want to prevent it from ever occurring.

Let's be clear here, communication does not equal confrontation. It is valid to fear having a conversation around hazing because you don't want to be singled out, considered an outsider, or being told you are wrong. It is the responsibility, however, for members to create and maintain a safe space for everyone in their chapter. Consider the benefits of communicating; you are considering the many levels of comfort and endorsing the importance of values. If it helps, try utilizing "I" terms and taking ownership (i.e., "I have noticed that the attitude of the chapter has shifted, and I don't feel the actions we are taking equate to our values"). It's not about who is wrong; it's about making sure it is made right. These conversations could be had with the President, New Member Educator, or Standards Officer, so that there is a way to set expectations, standards, and best practices for every member.

I know what you're thinking: there MUST still be a way to create healthy traditions within a chapter. You are correct, my friend! That tradition, however, should be inclusive to all and is open to edits and changes. Reassess the culture of your chapter with every new member class; maybe your chapter has never had a member who is Muslim and may have to consider the timing of your meetings. While I was a collegiate member, for example, we found that "the Wobble" was the song best associated with our chapter. It wasn't until we started dancing to it at Big Night (where all new members who accepted their invitation to membership came together to be welcomed into the chapter) where we had a new member quietly ask, "Are we being hazed to do this dance?" It made us realize that we were so used to this being a fun celebration but did not put into consideration how it might be perceived.

It's important to understand that there is a stigma with Greek Life, and we should not be enhancing stereotypes. Let us work on creating a world where fraternity and sorority are not associated with hazing, but with leadership and growth. That instead of asking "Were you hazed?", they can instead ask "Why was the Wobble your chapter song?"

Mel Lewis is a proud Charter member of Alpha Omicron Pi who has committed to Fraternal Movement and works within her passion for student development. As a first-generation college student, she attended Ramapo College of New Jersey for undergrad and achieved her Master's of Science in Education at Monmouth University. Mel has advised and worked with fraternity and sorority members from NIC, NPHC, NALFO, MGC, and NPC and has volunteered with her own organization since being initiated into alumna status. Mel transitioned from a campus-based professional to a headquarters staff and became the first Director of Education and Programs for Alpha Chi Rho National Fraternity. She thrives when she is working with students around mental health, growth, development, sexual violence, and inclusivity. She also holds the title for Most Likely to Defend New Jersey!

You can see Mel's presentations at
www.greekuniversity.org/mel

Email Mel: melissa@greekuniversity.org

CHAPTER 6

Considering Identity during New Member Education

Robert L. Wilson

T ake a moment to think back to your fraternity or sorority recruitment experience. Unsure how to dress, what to say, or how to act, you moved from house to house, room to room, or maybe even table to table, looking for connection or simply hoping that connection would find you. You were going through a staged process to achieve something which throughout most of human history has been determined by birth. You were navigating identity to find your tribe.

Our desire to find our tribe, whether it be within our fraternity or sorority experience, our friends outside our organization, our work groups in class, or even after school, when we enter the workforce, is a throwback to the earlier days of our evolution. Humans are inherently tribal. It is how we have survived so long and evolved as a species. Throughout most of our evolution, different tribes actually represented physical danger to us. Fortunately, in today's world, tribe is far less a matter of life or death than it was thousands of years ago. But, as is true in many areas of our brain's design, the wiring in our brains has not caught up to today's human experience. This very normal wiring toward tribalism is why we often say that many of our diversity, equity, and inclusion challenges are "head" related and not necessarily "heart" related.

The result is that we still live in a world primarily based on tribalism: What race are we? What political affiliation do we identify with? What country or state or even town are we from? What were our schools we attended, our social class, or like experiences across gender and sexual orientation, or even something trivial like what sports teams do we root for? And these tribes make it much more difficult to build trust. In fact, they spawn distrust. We tend to distrust people from different tribes, and far too often even assume the worst until proven otherwise.

So how do we overcome our natural tendency to separate ourselves into different tribes? It starts with understanding the relationship between inclusion and identity. Inclusion starts with how we value each person's identity.

Identity begins with each person's uniqueness. Each of us as humans are unique in our own way. In a recent study published in the journal *Nature Genetics*, even identical twins have been found to have genetic differences which emerge early on in the embryonic process!

There are also internal and external dimensions to our identity. Internal dimensions are those parts of ourselves that are very difficult to change, like our race, sex, gender, height, or perhaps even our neurological characteristics. External dimensions of identity are parts of ourselves that we have a bit more control over. These might be where we live, what religion we are a part of, what schools we attend or what profession we choose. We may also have an organizational identity, like our role within an organization, where we fall in the hierarchy, our seniority or the chapter we belong to. When we mix all of these elements of who we are, we have the identity we carry with us as we move through our daily lives.

Therefore, how we think about and value our own identity and one another's identity drives our understanding of diversity, equity, and inclusion.

Think for a moment about how you might rank the three most important parts of your identity. Some of you may struggle with this because you haven't thought about how you define your identity. After giving it some thought, you may struggle to rank your identities because different parts of our identity may be important or even blend together depending on the situation and environment we find ourselves in. After some thought, you might include in your rankings your hometown, your faith, or your ethnicity. Each of us may include different parts of our identity and we may rank them differently and that's okay.

Now a word of caution. Some of you may be thinking, "I'm hard working," "I'm funny," or "I'm very nice" as the key features of your identity. While these things may be true, they are not quite what we're looking for in this thought exercise. Focus more on social dimensions like the internal and external dimensions described previously.

I'll share my top three identities: my Catholic faith, my race, and my educational background as an engineer, because I find that I try to apply logic to things in which there is very little logic to be applied!

Now think for a minute about your top three identities and why you chose them. What is it about your background or your lived experience up to this point that influences why you chose the three identities you picked?

My top identity is my Catholic faith and why goes back to my own family history. My grandmother was born in a small town in Mississippi called Senatobia during the height of the Jim Crow era of the US Deep South. Most of our family were poor sharecroppers in the Mississippi Delta region. African Americans were denied basic rights during this era like voting, and there were severe restrictions on when, what, and where our family could go or what we could do especially when it meant interacting directly with whites. As a result, most of the members of my family, including my grandmother, had little formal education. When she came of age, she decided to leave Mississippi, and she emigrated to Detroit where relatives who had already left Mississippi took her in. In the Motor City, in the 1950s and 1960s she flourished, eventually buying a popular diner during a time when there were many barriers to black people trying to own their own business. When my grandmother met my grandfather, who had also emigrated from Georgia because of Jim Crow persecution, they fell in love and married. When they began to have children, my grandmother, who was born Protestant, realized that the best schools in Detroit at the time were the Catholic schools. She also learned that if her family was Catholic, the children could go to school either free or at a deep discount. So she converted to Catholicism, in part to ensure her children had the best educational opportunities available to them as Black children in segregated Detroit.

As a kid I still vividly remember going to church with my grandmother. She would elbow me when she noticed me dozing off and make sure I was following along with the Mass when I seemed to be lost. It only took one momentary glare from her to get me back on track. My grandmother passed away years ago, but it is when I am in church that I feel closest to her and to all the other members of my family who struggled through the brutality of slavery and Jim Crow so that I might have the opportunities I have now. And it is not lost on me that a woman with little education, emphasized education in a way that continues to change the life trajectory of descendants she never conceived of.

That is my story. What is yours? What are your top three identities? Are they the same as mine? Are they in the same order? Even the order of our top three identities can matter in how we interact with one another. We make assumptions about how other people view their identity based on how we view our own.

Last year, I was asked to coach and mentor a young man who was having trouble at work. We'll call him Charlie.

Though Charlie was a strong performer, he was creating conflicts with coworkers around inclusion in the aftermath of the murder of George Floyd in May 2020. I decided to do the same activity with him around identity that I just described. As it turned out, Charlie's top identity was his Christian faith. I figured that was a good starting point for our sessions since we both ranked our faith at the top. When I told him about my top three and my personal story about my family upbringing, Charlie responded that he "doesn't see color" and that he wished we would all stop talking about color and race because it divides us. I politely interjected that he and I may be in conflict now because I had just shared with him that race was my number two identity and he had dismissed it. Charlie became very defensive and told me that I was overreacting and that my response and emphasis on race is why we are so divided as a country. I decided to take a different tact with Charlie. I suggested we reconsider the activity and my ranking and that we pretend I didn't place my Catholic faith as my number one. I followed that I didn't think we should be talking about religion, his number one. I explained that religion is divisive and that really, we are all one of God's children and a person's religious faith is unimportant. Well, Charlie became even more agitated. He raised his voice and reminded me that his religion is the most important part of who he is. He also told me that in today's society, he feels that he is attacked because of his Christian faith. He said he wanted to be respected for his faith and not dismissed when he expressed it.

This exchange between Charlie and me describes the foundation of where our identity conflicts originate. I told Charlie that we can't have it both ways. It can't be that when it is an aspect of identity that is important to him it needs to be respected but when it is an aspect of identity not important to him, we should avoid talking about it. I had made my point with Charlie.

Conflicts around identity are where our diversity and inclusion challenges begin. Why these conflicts happen harkens back to a quote I love from the late, great management guru, Stephen R. Covey. "We think we see the world the way it is, when in fact we see the world as we are."[56] I first heard this quote years ago while facilitating a Franklin Covey workshop and it has stayed with me. We have a window or lens through which we see the world. And we make assumptions about other people based on what has been put on our window or lens to the world. And our window or lens is impacted by our experiences, like who raised us, where we were raised, our education, who we surround ourselves with, where we have traveled, traditional and social media, and the traumas we have endured. All of these things play into our sense of identity. And our sense of identity impacts how we interact with other people and move through the world each day.

Tribalism, and how we think about and value our own identity and one another's identity, drives our challenges around diversity, equity, and inclusion.

---

[56] https://resources.franklincovey.com/mkt-7hv1/paradigms-src

Robert Lawrence Wilson is a speaker, facilitator, and writer with expertise in diversity and inclusion, multicultural outreach marketing and leadership development. Cofounder of the Culture Shift Team, he leads their diversity strategy development and training across all platforms and markets from higher education and nonprofit to corporate.

Robert began his journey in diversity and inclusion as an undergraduate at the University of Michigan, where he served as a residence hall diversity peer advisor. He has served in executive roles at Nissan North America, including as the company's first Director of Diversity and Inclusion and as Director of Customer Experience. He developed and led Nissan's diversity practice and multicultural market strategy for the Americas.

Robert serves on the leadership boards of several nonprofit organizations promoting greater access to quality education for the nation's most at-risk student population. He is also cofounder of the Tennessee Diversity Consortium. Robert holds a Bachelor's Degree in Mechanical Engineering from the University of Michigan and a Master's Degree in Business Administration from Duke University.

You can see Robert's presentations at:
www.greekuniversity.org/robert

Email Robert: robert@greekuniversity.org

Expanding Membership Development and Connection by Supporting a Culture of Mental Health

Greg Vogt

As we think about the approach of new member development, we often turn to certain aspects of the Greek experience that have been relied upon over time. Such things may include Ritual, history of the organization, values, academic benchmarks, among others. These focuses remain important when fostering an effective process among new members. In addition, there is a wonderful opportunity that exists for fraternities and sororities to prioritize.

This opportunity is the importance of building connection and belonging among new members. Rather than relying on the routines we're used to, we must also have a vision for creating trust and genuine friendship within and across the organization.

A question to consider may be, "Why are things like connection and belonging important for membership development?" This alone, sets the stage for the strategies we'll explore putting in place to bring members together. Brené Brown, one of the world's prolific researchers on vulnerability, has uncovered significant findings. Through over two decades of research, her work concludes that joy, connection, and belonging are at the core of every decision and desire an individual has. Perhaps this is why we join Greek organizations in the first place: to connect, to belong, to find joy.

Brown goes on to explain that vulnerability is the key method to build a culture of joy, connection, and belonging. When looking at this further, an overarching narrative to expand membership development is supporting a culture of mental health. Focusing on mental health doesn't just go for the initial pledge process, but would be more beneficial to create longevity throughout the tenure of a student's time in college.

The Importance of Mental Health for Membership Development

Creating a supportive culture of mental health in our fraternities and sororities takes a collaborative and individual effort. It is a goal that can't be achieved in a day, and rather, should be understood as an approach with a long-term consistent effort.

Mental health, as defined by the National Council of Behavioral Health, is "a state of well-being in which an individual realizes their own abilities, can cope with normal stressors of life, can work productively and fruitfully, and contributes to their community."

Mental health commands our focus and intentionality each day of our lives. We may be struggling with a challenge currently, or may at some point in the future. At the very least, we all know at least one person in our sphere of influence who is struggling with a mental health challenge currently—someone who is in need of support. A helpful reference of this is the *Mental Health Continuum.* This chart breaks down the five zones of mental health: in crisis, struggling, surviving, thriving, excelling. We all know people who fall into each of these respective descriptions that come with different feelings and symptoms. In fact, we're all likely to enter into each of these zones at some point during our lives, and quite possibly during a student's time in college. This is another reason why mental health education, resources, and discussions should be considered a priority throughout the entire college experience.

This is why it matters. Because we have an opportunity to support one another, and certainly during an experience such as membership development. Building real connection among members is critical to the long-term health of the organization and retention. Fostering relationships through a focus on mental health can prevent cliques from forming, tension, and resentment across the group. Individually, it certainly will play a role in the well-being of each student. When researching the relationship between mental health and fraternity and sorority membership, Good Therapy found a positive correlation. "Student success is directly impacted by the sense of belonging, defined as membership, feelings of acceptance, being cared about, or part of a group."[57]

We have a responsibility to keep this at the forefront during membership development, which can be viewed not just as a semester-long focus, but rather the entirety of a student's college career. We are always evolving, learning, and adapting. New challenges present a demand to keep mental health at the forefront throughout college, not just in the beginning of joining Greek Life. Feelings of achievement, belonging, and connection mean that each member feels cared for, included, and welcomed. Individually, each person should know the contribution opportunity they have within the fraternity or sorority. Collectively, the group should maintain a focus on supporting mental health to build the culture within the organization, but also, to help change the narrative on what we're seeing on campuses today.

Statistics as a Challenge and Opportunity

College students, whether Greek or not, are currently experiencing significant mental health challenges. Active Minds, the nation's premier non-profit organization for

---

[57] Karen Osterman, "Students' Need for Belonging in the School Community" (2000) quoted by Kendall Coffman, "Fraternity and Sorority Membership for College Students," GoodTherapy, https://www.goodtherapy.org/blog/College-Students-Belonging-Benefits-of-Fraternity-Sorority-Membership?fbclid=IwAR1oXMIff1hGDK3szlv1BYqu0-HXEDZV_jsUefqIPdcHWkXaUuVn8cBBBuw.

mental health on college campuses, has published recent
findings including the following:

- Suicide is the second leading cause of death among
  young adults
- 75% of mental health issues begin by age 24
- 39% of college students experience a significant
  mental health issue
- 67% of people between 18–24 with anxiety or
  depression don't seek treatment[58]

The unfortunate reality is that students are having a difficult
time for various reasons. Cigna conducted a national survey
of over 10,000 responders on loneliness. They found that 79%
of Gen Z admitted to feeling lonely, the highest out of any
generation.[59] As loneliness tears through college campuses,
fraternities and sororities have an opportunity to change that
void. Not just by having an organization for students to plug
into, but by creating thoughtful programming on improving
the membership development process, and therefore,
meaningful connection.

Perspectives from Lived Experience

To make this come to life a bit more, I'd like to share three
stories with you. The first was during a time when I was
disconnected and lonely, having a negative effect on my
mental health.

---

[58] https://www.activeminds.org/about-mental-health/statistics/

[59] "Loneliness and the Workplace," Cigna.com, 2020, https://www.cigna.
com/static/www-cigna-com/docs/about-us/newsroom/studies-and-reports/
combatting-loneliness/cigna-2020-loneliness-factsheet.pdf.

When I was sixteen years old, I didn't make the high school basketball team. I was having challenges building friendships and relationships. I went to class, but just went through the motions. I lacked direction and purpose. I hit a place of stagnation. This seems somewhat normal, doesn't it? Nothing completely out of the ordinary? Well, that's an accurate depiction, but a situation that can't be neglected or brushed over. The reason being is that these circumstances, when not dealt with properly, created a downward spiral behaviorally. Since my core friend group was through basketball, I lost my support system. My confidence diminished and my willingness to try new things such as clubs, groups, or other sports depleted. Disconnection and loneliness became normal because I didn't have the right friends or coping mechanisms in place to help me move forward and keep me accountable. I began to isolate rather than invest in friendships. I began to blame others, rather than taking responsibility myself. I retreated from challenge rather than choosing to embrace it. Eventually, circumstances turned into a lifestyle and framework of thinking. I was isolated. I was lonely. I was anxious. I was depressed. And when it became too much to bear, I became convinced that suicide was the only option.

In this slice of my story, my hope is that you see the opportunity for an outsider to come in to provide support in a situation like this. Certainly, Greek organizations, with the right approach and people, can be a source to support and redirect someone in a situation like this while at college.

The second story follows in a season of life directly after two suicide attempts in high school. I was sent out of state to a residential treatment center for twelve months. I could spend hours listing the challenges that came with this transition, but instead of doing so, let's look at what was in place: two things. First, a depressed, sixteen-year-old who lost his passion for life and ended up at rehab. Second, a facility grounded in fostering a culture of mental health through its people, therapy, and resources.

Through consistent counseling, peer-to-peer support, a new understanding of vulnerability, and listening to wise council, I had the system in place to improve and get back on track. I didn't necessarily conquer every challenge I had or even depression during that year, but I walked out of that facility a different person than I had entered. I was full again. I had clear thinking again. I had people in my circle again. I had connection again. I had hope again.

Even with members or students who are struggling right now, do you see what a wonderful opportunity we have to meet them where they're at to support? Sure, it may not be a treatment center, but through the right approaches that Greek Life and new membership provides, we can make a difference in the lives of our members and their development.

The third story is a look into what Greek Life did for me. I went to the University of Arizona just months after getting discharged from the residential treatment center. I wasn't like the other kids. I didn't have a prom. I couldn't play sports senior year. I couldn't go to parties or dances. Though I improved mentally through my time in treatment, to say I was nervous going to college was an understatement. I felt behind everyone else around me in nearly all aspects of life. During those first couple weeks of college, I was walking on eggshells, confused, and faking it to the max. But things changed once my freshman roommate convinced me to explore Greek Life. I ended up joining a fraternity, and the experience did leaps and bounds for my development. I met new people from different backgrounds, got to be part of something bigger than myself, tried new things I normally wouldn't try, received mentorship, and developed a support system that was authentic and always present. The fraternal experience expanded my way of thinking. Through the men who were leaders in our organization, the stage was set for us new members. They focused not just on "fun," but more so on the realness of the experience. They created opportunities for us to share in authentic ways. They created a culture that was welcoming and made it known that if there was personal trouble for any reason, we know where we could go for direction and support. One of the ways the organization was most effective was how intentional they were in making sure each member knew one another on a deep, personal level. It created a culture of honesty, realness, and transparency. We knew much of the good, the bad, and the ugly of one another, but that's what made our fraternity thrive and made us individually feel like we had a family at college. This fostered the willingness to show up for one another during difficult times.

I believe that each fraternity, sorority, and council have this opportunity. Regardless of where it was founded, how many members are present, how popular it is on campus, or whatever else, each organization has an opportunity to enhance membership development by supporting a culture of mental health.

The 4 P's: Membership Development Initiatives for Your Organization

We've reviewed the importance of mental health, challenges students are facing, and the opportunities that arise for Greek organizations to step in to foster a priority on mental health during the membership process. I'd now like to leave you with a simple roadmap that you may consider following as your chapter approaches new membership. "The 4 P's" can serve as a simple framework, or pillars of focus, during the membership process when it comes to supporting each member's mental health. Only the leaders of the organization know exactly what the specific opportunities are to improve for that respective chapter, but my hope is that this can help create an effective membership process by focusing on connection, belonging, and mental health.

People

The first pillar here is to not neglect a chapter's biggest asset: its people. Having a consistent focus on the members themselves, and their development, will yield great results. There are several other people groups that can be focused upon to aid in this process. First, is making sure there are honest, genuine, selfless leaders in the chapter to lead by example. Having an executive board that understands the benefit of genuine connection among members is vital. A board that cares about the individual just as much as the collective group as a whole will go a long way in developing membership. Another people resource to consider is connecting with the national office. Determining what support is needed and having the willingness to ask for help on a greater level will have positive impacts at the local level when done appropriately. A final aspect to consider is having trusted individuals who are outside of the organization. Who is outside of the chapter that needs to have a voice with the chapter, or with an individual? Perhaps it is a campus counselor or therapist. Perhaps it is a guest speaker or advisor. Perhaps it is a council leader or FSL employee. Maybe it's local alumni. The key is to seek support from all people groups—in house, corporate, and out of house.

| *Practices*

When it comes to pouring into our greatest asset, our people, the next step to ask is how do we do so? What are the practices or strategies to build a culture of belonging, trust, and real friendship? There are several ways to think about this, none better than having the members talk about it. Put the ball in their court and ask; what would be helpful for you? How can we make this an enriched experience for you where you feel valued? What ways do you see we can improve building connection among members? As great as it is to have effective leadership, sometimes the best approach is listening to the needs of the people themselves, in this case, new or existing members. Some specific ideas may include arranging events within the chapter to get to know one another on more meaningful levels, breaking into smaller groups for conversations, activities, and storytelling, team-building activities that command trust and communication, etc. The best way to foster this environment is to get behind a member or two who feel comfortable being vulnerable

themselves and letting them set the tone of the conversation
or event, no matter the subject matter. Other practices that
may be useful when fostering a culture of mental health
include encouraging sports and recreational activity, event
planning that requires teamwork and each person to have
a unique role, group study sessions, etc. And certainly,
encouraging students to utilize the campus counseling center
when appropriate.

Places

The next pillar to keep in mind when thinking about
engaging membership development is the places that are at
our fingertips to serve as a benefit or resource. This is not
to be overcomplicated, but rather, ask, which places nearby
can be of positive use to individual members or the group
as a whole? Certainly, let's not overlook the fraternity or
sorority house itself. All effort must begin there. Beyond that
though, there are plenty of places that can be resourceful;
campus recreation center, campus counseling center, campus
Active Minds chapter, a friends' apartment or dorm room,
favorite sport arena, favorite restaurant, a local church,
nearby volunteer and serving centers, nature that is accessible
to campus, etc. All of these may seem simple, but they reap
great dividends for individuals and chapters as a whole when
utilized to manage mental health, de-stress, and build a sense
of community among the places we have access to.

Practical Resources

Finally, practical resources involve seeking out tangible support when needed. This may be on or off campus. This may be help on a small issue, or emergencies during a crisis. Regardless, it's critically important to have this be the top focus among each individual member and the chapter all together. Perhaps, making a bulletin board in the house or creating a Cloud document to source each of these for member reference would be beneficial. These are certainly just the tip of the iceberg, and support should be sought by what that particular person's needs are. This list is a general overview, and not a formal recommendation, but more so food for thought. Below are a few mental health resources that college students may find helpful:

- On-campus counseling center
- NAMI: https://nami.org/Home
- American Foundation for Suicide Prevention: https://afsp.org
- *Psychology Today* ("Find a Therapist" link): https://www.psychologytoday.com/us
- Active Minds (student-led mental health chapter): https://www.activeminds.org
- Depression and Bipolar Support Alliance: https://www.dbsalliance.org
- National Suicide Prevention Lifeline: 1(800) 273-8255
- Crisis Text Line: Text HOME to 741741

My hope is that by understanding the challenges students face and realizing that we all have a commonality in having mental health, our chapters can work on supporting membership development with a greater emphasis on mental health. I've seen firsthand how a positive Greek Life experience can improve well-being and belonging. I encourage each chapter and member to embrace the challenge and responsibility. There is much to be said about a chapter that operates with a together-first mentality, yet at the same time, one that facilitates the support of each member when it comes to their personal mental health. Not every conversation will be easy. There will be times of struggle and discomfort. But a healthy chapter is one that focuses on mental health and connection among its members, not by aiming for perfection, but by constantly showing up and being present for one another.

Greg Vogt is a Professional Mental Health Speaker with Greek University and is Mental Health First Aid Certified. He also speaks in partnership with Active Minds, the nation's premier nonprofit organization for mental health among young adults. Greg is the author of *The Battle Against Yourself*, and serves as a Board Member for the Depression & Bipolar Support Alliance (California). His keynote addresses include mental health during life transitions, suicide prevention, strategies to start a conversation, and how to seek support.

You can see Greg's presentations at:
www.greekuniversity.org/greg

Email Greg: greg@greekuniversity.org

CHAPTER 8

My Legacy Is Not Your Legacy

Pietro A. Sasso

The role of a legacy in their sorority or fraternity is often a vaunted or special status applied to someone who has a unique relationship to their fraternal organization. They have a biological relationship to someone who is already a member, such as their mother or father. Legacies are often assumed to be an "always joiner" because they have been socialized to hear about sorority or fraternity experiences from their family. This facilitates some pressures and maybe even some confusion about the role of a legacy.

Social movements such as #AbolishGreekLife or other social equity movements among undergraduate college students have challenged the legitimacy of the legacy system and the privileges of automatic membership invitations. In particular, sororities have been challenged to reconsider this status because legacy women members often take space away from other members. Opponents of the legacy system suggest that it inhibits diversity and inclusion and perpetuates elitism. Additionally, some legacy sorority members may feel pressure to affiliate and conform to their fraternal legacy. This chapter will preset my story as a legacy in my own organization as well some additional considerations readers of this chapter may want to examine when recruiting, supporting, and affiliating legacy members.

Defining Legacies

There has been significant debate about the *legacy system* across the larger national sorority and fraternity community. Historically, a *legacy* was someone who was a direct familial descendant of a member. This typically was a father or mother. However, as fraternities and sororities advanced and evolved, it was not uncommon for a fraternity or sorority "legacy" membership to include aunts, uncles, and grandparents. In many fraternities, especially in culturally-based organizations such as with the National Panhellenic Conference (NPC), there are *generational legacies*.

Generational legacies often include a at least three generations of membership in the same organization or even chapter. A grandparent, a parent, and now the current student are all proud members of the same sorority or fraternity. The role and influence of a legacy is different between sororities and fraternities.

In sororities, the role of the legacy receives much less influence, but might be celebrated with informal rites of passage. Some sororities have informal ceremonies for legacy members in which the family members pass down their pin or badge. However, legacy members often still count toward total membership and do not receive any special preferences toward membership in some sororities unfortunately. Many sororities such as those in NPC have eliminated preferential bidding for legacy members.

In culturally-based sororities, a legacy woman may receive more preferred treatment or an automatic bid for membership. Due to the cultural heritage of these organizations, legacies often suggest distinctive familial ties, traditions, and patterns of cultural transmission. This influences the identity development of these student legacy members.

In fraternities, the role of the legacy suggests masculinity and virility. The role of the legacy to many grandfathers or fathers is that their descendent is carrying on their family name in their fraternity and in their general life. They are all walking in the same footsteps in their undergraduate collegiate experience. Thus, it can connect men together across generations which often can be fraught with some tensions. However, legacy membership, like with sororities, often means more within the family system than it does within the organization. Legacy membership in a fraternity does not come with any special privileges beyond automatic membership. Fraternities often have greater autonomy in selecting their members and do not have a ceiling on chapter membership size, and will traditionally offer automatic invitations to legacies. Some organizations have traditions in which the badge, pin, or other membership costs might be waived for legacy members as a way to encourage their affiliation.

Within culturally-based fraternities, the role of the legacy often holds greater responsibility and they are often assumed to be a chapter leaders. There might be increased pressure to assume a leadership role and exceed the levels of involvement of their forefathers. Culturally-based fraternities will also offer automatic membership to legacy members. Also, if there is an inactive chapter on their campus, legacy members are often contacted to reactivate the chapter with a new founding line. This was my experience as a legacy founder of my chapter.

My Story as a Legacy

As one can discern from my name, I am from Latino, Italian, and Middle Eastern descent, and I identify strongly with my cultural heritage. Thus, the influence of culture is important to me in considering my fraternity affiliation. Only my father attended college within my immediate family and he was an immigrant from Europe. He attended Rutgers University-Newark and affiliated with Tau Delta Phi Fraternity in a chapter primarily comprised of Italian American and Latino immigrants. He never initially pushed me to join his fraternity, but encouraged me to affiliate with one. None of my sisters or my mother attended college, so my only support was from my father who had graduated college more than forty years prior. While I was not a first-generation student, it often felt like a very parallel experience. My father instilled an extraordinarily strong commitment to a blue-collar work ethic and a focus on education, which is how he escaped extreme poverty as a young man. So he held a retrospective appreciation for the social and cultural capital his fraternity chapter provided to him, which he cited was the primary reasons he persisted to graduation in college. Thus, I did not quite understand what I was getting into when joining a fraternity. I only had popular media and the experiences of my father to understand the collegiate fraternity experience.

In much of my pre-college experience I struggled with speech disfluency and cultural identity diffusion. I suffered from a moderate stutter and confusion about how I should identify. I am Latino, but many times others confused with where I fit in. I did not feel like I had ever "been enough" to anyone and I wanted to belong. I desired to find a sense of belonging and really wanted to join any fraternity. I did not consider factors such as values or making friends within the chapter. I went through the formal recruitment process my freshman year and then I made a very costly miscalculation. It was actually a huge mistake.

For my undergraduate experience, I attended a distinctly Southern liberal arts college. It was here that I initially affiliated with a fraternity my freshman year. I joined because I thought they were "cool" and were the largest chapter on campus with seventy members. There was such a diverse spectrum of personalities and experiences, I thought I would fit in somewhere within the spectrum of all of them. I really struggled to find my own space within their chapter culture. My preliminary undergraduate fraternity experience was traumatic and a disaster.

I was severely hazed, in that I was subjected to forced alcohol consumption, snorting grain alcohol, physical restraints, calisthenics, and even huffing human waste. The late-night group hazing experiences accumulated a negative impact on my grades—and if I had not disassociated, I think I would have failed some of my courses. My grades dropped significantly regardless, but I disassociated from the fraternity which resulted in threats and verbal harassment when I walked around campus. I felt like a failure once again. I developed a close group of friends outside of my fraternity and almost lost my associations with them because of all the time I committed toward my "pledging" experience.

My father eventually suggested that maybe I should start my own fraternity. After conversations with a trusted campus advisor, I felt that this would be a great idea. Here was an opportunity for me to experience leadership and finally feel "enough." Unbeknownst to me, many of my peers were looking for a similar sense of belonging, especially after I had ignored them several times in my first attempt with fraternity affiliation. Five of my friends and I decided to form the Alpha class and began our own chapter and it grew eventually. It became a recognized organization on campus and within the campus IFC. However, this occurred not without significant struggle.

In the tradition of my fraternity, we have "scroll list" which is the alpha order of initiation. As a legacy founder, I was "scroll one" and then assigned to be the chapter president or "consul." I was ready to be a legacy founder of a chapter, but not a chapter president. The student paper ran a story about me with a headline suggesting I was merely "looking for more friends," which invalidated my experiences and the legitimacy of the chapter I sought to construct with my peers. Despite these initial challenges and confusion, the chapter eventually began with six young men who later became my brothers.

The chapter was disruptive to the campus fraternity/sorority community because it was one of the first totally inclusive fraternities at the university. Remember the context in which this is occurring. This is immediately right after 9/11, Nelly and Ja Rule are dominating the radio, unfortunately with Nickelback. This was still a Southern predominantly white institution (PWI). None of the founders were traditionally white, as the chapter was founded by one biracial, two mixed-heritage Latinos, and three Black men. Later, many openly gay and other student leaders of color joined our founding group of fifteen that all became the names on the chapter charter.

The reaction by others was unsupportive and largely falling along lines of *white silence* and avoidance. While we may have been disruptive to the campus climate, the NPC sororities did not immediately want to hold social events with us, and others felt that our chapter did not need to exist. This phenomenon called *white immunity* occurred because white students were insulated from this disparate treatment and struggled to conceptualize a chapter with significant intersectional social identities. The outcome was that the campus Interfraternity Council refused to encourage our participation and recognition as a student organization. So the chapter operated *sub rosa* for almost two academic years until student affairs professionals eventually intervened to support our pleas for campus recognition.

My experience as a legacy founder was mostly advocating for the inclusion of my campus sorority/fraternity community in integrating our chapter of Tau Delta Phi. This occurred twenty years ago, and much of what I experienced have remained issues today in the contemporary context. This chapter was more than 40 percent students of color and the majority were first-generation students on federal financial aid. More than a third were gay or queer-identified cisgendered men. The chapter maintained this demographic composition for some time after I graduated, but eventually moved backward toward integration of the student community norms. The chapter still was inclusive of a significant number of LGBTQ-identified students throughout its existence. Unfortunately, the chapter eventually faded into obscurity due to lack of membership as other chapters integrated their membership. Our chapter lost its purpose and never could reconceptualize a new mission. Even so, these experiences were formative and provided a sense of belonging when no other fraternal organizations open their doors.

Being a legacy offered me a new opportunity to have a positive fraternity experience. I probably would have not affiliated with another chapter, particularly after my experiences with terrible hazing. I gained experience founding a fraternity chapter, disrupting campus culture, and providing space to those placed between the margins by various systems of oppression. Their identities were invisible to administrators at my undergraduate institution that was a PWI. My fraternity legacy experience provided me with a sense of belonging, social capital, and leadership experiences in a campus environment. I also learned concepts of healthy or productive masculinities. My experiences with other college men from different backgrounds beyond my mixed Latino heritage changed my perspectives toward education, equity, and acceptance of difference. I saw issues of marginality, internalized racism, and experienced some parallel experiences of my own. I learned these are issues I want to combat across our educational systems.

After college, I took a position with my fraternity for a year as a leadership consultant and later progressed to serve the fraternity's Executive Council as National Vice President. I developed amazing friendships and traveled the East Coast starting additional chapters in a similar vein and image as my undergraduate chapter focused on creating belonging and inclusivity. I successfully oversaw the founding and chartering of five chapters. Being a legacy and my fraternity experience allowed me to find my career in higher education. These experiences positioned me to engage in sorority/fraternity research and become a scholar in this area as a college professor. I have educated and supported the professional preparation of a number of sorority/fraternity professionals and I tell them a very similar story the ones contained within these pages.

I was fortunate that my father's brotherhood in Tau Delta Phi did not cast a significant shadow. However, I did self-impose some internal pressures which I created for myself. I felt a pressure to define my own legacy as a founder and continue the one my father established. Our fraternity member did not bring us closer together as father and son, but rather it helped me empathize to walk in the shoes of my father as a college student. I better understood how his fraternity experience shaped his machismo masculinity. Such an experience taught me I can continue a legacy, but can redefine it too. The shadow I cast, like my legacy, was not my father's, but my own.

Defining Your Own Legacy

As a college professor and researcher of sororities and fraternities, I have a few perspectives on some trends I suggest you advocate for on your campus to promote the role of legacy membership.

1) Legacies Promote Cultural Transmission

My organization, Tau Delta Phi, is a culturally-based organization and is one of the smallest NIC member organization in the country. We have always struggled to communicate our worth. However, as a small organization we have many legacies that join and become chapter leaders. The majority of our members are first-generation students from diverse communities. Thus, the fraternity is a place of cultural transmission which builds social capital. This is a transformative experience. On your campus, legacy membership is particularly important as an opportunity for sense of belonging and connectedness. Other organizations and chapters tend to overlook many students of color or they are intimidated to affiliate because of the assumptions or lack of inclusion in our communities. However, legacies offer an opportunity for change and inclusion. This means your national organization, or your own chapter, should communicate regularly with your alumni/ae to get referrals for any legacies coming to your chapter. Reach out to them and communicate the value of legacy membership.

2) Legacies Connect Generations

My fraternity experience did not bring my father and I closer as I mentioned before. There were two generations between us as he was significantly older than I. However, it did help me understand my father much more and empathize with his own collegiate undergraduate experience. There is value in legacy membership connecting generations. Legacy membership may connect Baby Boomers, Xers, and Millennials to Gen Z students. Despite all the student calls for inclusion and external calls for reform, the sorority and fraternity experience maintains a sense of history through its Ritual. This Ritual is the rite of passage, and its esotericism and secrecy binds generations together. Legacies should speak to their family members who affiliated as well about their chapter to learn how they experienced this as a fraternity or sorority member. This sense of history creates a pride in continuing a familial legacy which may become a tradition. If I have a son, I would love for him to join Tau Delta Phi. Even if I have a daughter, I want her to "Go Greek." Joining such a ubiquitous college experience facilitates a larger legacy of participation and contribution to the sorority or fraternity movement.

3) Legacies Increase Membership

Legacies typically make great fraternity men and sorority women. However, as a legacy member myself, I often struggle with how we devalue them. There is distinction regarding how sororities and fraternities facilitate recruitment of legacies. In NPC sororities, they count toward the overall membership totals and then they are often not allowed to write down if they are a legacy member on some campuses. Other NPC sororities have disallowed preferences for legacy members. Sorority chapters and recruitment counselors are often discouraged from asking about legacy membership as well in formal recruitment. Sorority legacies can really openly discuss their status in continuous open bidding or during informal recruitment. In NIC organizations or other culturally-based fraternities and sororities, legacies remain an important component of chapter membership and are typically offered an invitation for membership. There has to be a compelling argument or rationale to deny membership to a legacy in many fraternities. If you are a chapter leader, I encourage you to advocate for their rights in sororities and to actively recruit them in fraternities or other culturally-based organizations.

4) Define Your Own Legacy

Since my father was not terribly involved in my fraternity experience, I self-imposed my own pressures as a legacy founder of my chapter. However, many legacies may have pressure from their family members who are also sorority or fraternity members to be a model chapter leader. Even if you are a legacy, it does not define you. You need to define your own legacy and cast your own shadow rather than that of your family members. Their history and contributions matter, but you will write your own. You can change and advocate just as I did for change in your chapter of your own sorority or fraternity community.

Conclusion

Legacy membership in a fraternity or sorority continues as a historical narrative and tradition. Many suggest it is elitism and exclusionary, but many counternarratives such as my own exist. If you are not a legacy, consider intentionally recruiting them. If you are a legacy, you will need to self-author your own narrative in which you can make your own historical legacy. It is my hope that by reading this brief chapter you will consider how the legacy system of sororities and fraternities has changed. There are significant complexities, but it adds sophistication and history to our fraternal community. It suggests to us that we are a part of a system of rich tradition that extends generations into families. We need to write our own legacies and offer a new hope to redefine the sorority and fraternity experience.

Dr. Pietro A. Sasso is an author, researcher, and professor of higher education/student affairs. His research centers the voices of college students and is the senior curator of several text series. He is also generally very vocal across social media and has made numerous public discourse contributions within the media. He is currently a research fellow at the Piazza Center for Fraternity & Sorority Research and Reform.

Dr. Pietro A. Sasso has over fifteen years of professional and teaching experience in postsecondary education. As an administrator, his experience is exceptionally diverse, spanning several educational administrative functional areas. In each of these functional areas, Pietro has been provided with increasing levels of responsibility which demands various levels of leadership. He has provided significant culture change and improvements to each of his areas of accountability. He is also a research-scholar with significant experiences as an educator and academic advisor to both undergraduate and graduate students. His research interests include the college experience (student involvement, multiraciality, masculinity), student success (academic advising, student persistence), and educational equity across co-curricular spaces.

You can learn more about Dr. Sasso at: www.drsasso.com

Email Dr. Sasso: pietro.sasso@sfasu.edu

CHAPTER 9

Making Connections between Existing and New Members

Cassie Perry, Edson O'Neale, Tricia Benitez

Cassie Perry: Connect with Members

Think about the last really great book you read (aside from our first Greek University publication *Creating Impact on Your College Campus and Beyond after From Letters to Leaders*: of course). What made you want to turn to the next page or explore the next chapter to see where the story led? Maybe it was your connection to the character development or the plot was thickening.

When I need to take a break from my crazy busy life, one of my favorite hobbies is to read. I also love to watch movies! Every fall I look forward to the movie *Hocus Pocus* as it pops up on Netflix. Aside from the nostalgia of my childhood giddiness surrounding Halloween, as an adult I get all the feels from the greater lesson of encouraging love, courage, and bonds of a family—while also celebrating the individuality within. Maybe it's the "potion" we all need to drink from a little more these days?

As the lead character in the story of our life—and also as a supporting one in our fraternity or sorority—we have an opportunity to shine in both roles. As our own Greek "chapters" continue to be written and grow, it begs the question, How do we continue to engage our existing members and also create inclusivity and a feeling of importance to our new or potential ones?

Here are a few ideas:

1. Defined and dedicated rituals—new and old
2. Creating personal connection/ engagement in chapter meetings
3. Sharing/collaborating our personal goals

It's Not a Spell; It's a Ritual

Rituals are a vital part of any fraternity or sorority. They are traditions that are shared not only with many generations of students in an individual chapter, but they also unite that chapter to their much larger national roots and founders. Instituting a few new ones that are individual to your campus chapter is another way to bond in the present—and secure friendships for life.

Some of my most memorable nights as a member of Pi Beta Phi at Indiana University were celebrating our big sis/little sis tradition. As a new pledge, our "cauldron," if you will, is often mixed with feelings of excitement for all that is to come, a little anxiety, and a pinch or two of insecurity. We all arrive to bid night with a desire to be included and part of something bigger—yet recognized for the unique and special qualities that we were ultimately chosen for.

This is a time when there is nothing "Little" about being a "Big."

The pictures we see on social media celebrating these occasions often show off matching sweatshirts, posed cheek-to-cheek pictures and hashtags swathed in adoration. However, this tradition is so much more than 1,000 likes or a branded pledge paddle interlocking your names for life. It's an opportunity to be a mentor in both moments of success and failure—in and outside of the four walls of your Greek house. It's a chance to have someone you feel is your person, your chosen sister/brother to look to for guidance and support as you turn the page on a new chapter in your life and subsequently as the years go by, a chance for you to be that person to someone else.

Chapter Meetings: Stir in a Little UNsocial Distancing

This is typically one hour that your entire house becomes a "home." A time to share news, ideas, celebrate one another's wins . . . and support a few unfortunate losses that are bound to have happened throughout the week. For sixty minutes you have the opportunity to engage with this entire chosen family as a whole. Aside from the obvious business part of the meeting—these minutes are not just meant to be recorded in a binder—they are also intended for connectivity.

In order to foster more personal engagement between members, perhaps . . .

- At the beginning of the meeting, everyone grabs a little slip of paper on their way in. Take a dedicated moment before the meeting is called to order to write a kind message for another member and pass along in a communal bowl of sorts. Perhaps this is a compliment to someone else, or even a request for prayer or thought for yourself as you find yourself in a time of struggle and need extra support. At the end of the meeting, the president will read them aloud to the entire chapter—therefore essentially ending one week and beginning another on a positive note of encouragement and solidarity.
- Another idea might be to pass the gavel around the room and share a positive story or potentially a nomination for "sister or brother of the week" (and why that member should be celebrated for their impact in the community or for representing the values of their organization).
- If your chapter has more of a private feel, a nice way to accomplish both of these ideas is to hang a bulletin board where members can post/tack either or all of the above and appoint someone to update weekly.

Sip and Gain Nourishment from the Same Cup (unless we are still in a pandemic, that is) by Sharing Your Goals

Goals based on shared values or mutual interests tend to deepen the bond of trust between people. Whether these are aimed at success at school or future career, or more personally or emotionally based, often times we discover that our goals are not all that individual in theory at all. Identifying others that are working toward similar milestones creates an accountable support network and only helps to further our chances of success. Similarly, if we determine and engage a mentor who has set out to achieve the same goal—not only can we learn from their accomplishment—more often than not we are gifted to also learn from the stumbles they undoubtedly had along the way.

So where to start?

- Much like the Little/Big tradition, identify and incorporate member matches who share similar academic interests, career choice and/or personal goals such as leading a healthier lifestyle.
- Dedicate monthly break-out sessions (perhaps after a chapter meeting) to share ideas, accomplishments/setbacks and set new goals.
- Open up. Like really . . . open up. Get vulnerable and don't be afraid to admit when you feel like you might be failing. Everyone has been there. Know you're not alone and are not being judged but rather admired for the strength it takes to keep

working toward your goals amidst the challenges that arise.

No matter what, don't lose sight of the fact we all bring our own magic to the world. By stirring our unique chapters together, we can collectively create a story of genuine connection and unity . . . in our Greek years and beyond.

Edson O'Neale: Serve the Community

As a freshman in college, coming all the way from the Virgin Islands, I made it my goal to be a part of something big, where I could make an impact on campus and the community. While trying to "find myself," I came across a fraternity that piqued my interest. I was a little hesitant at first because I did not know much about fraternities. To be honest, I did not know anything at all about fraternities other than what they showed on television, but I decided to give it a shot. As I got to know the members of that respective chapter, I definitely saw myself being a part of that organization, but I was unsure if they wanted me. I got to know the members, and surprisingly, I was invited to a party. I thought this would be a great way to get to know the members of the chapter. Ain't nothing better than getting to know people at a party!

We drove to the club where the party was being held and as we got there the atmosphere was just amazing. I was introduced to so many people and really began to feel like I belonged. The DJ was on point playing some great music, and I even got the chance to dance with girls. I was so shy, but the atmosphere, support, and friendliness of the brothers brought something out of me that made me feel comfortable and accepted. After the party ended, we drove back to campus and talked about how much fun we had. It was very late, or very early depending on how you see it, and I started heading back to my dorm room when one of the members asked me, "Oh by the way, you coming to Community Service in the morning with us, right?" I was surprised by the invitation and also had no idea what he was talking about, so to play it off I asked, "What time?" Then he responded, "Six a.m., meet us in our dorm room, and we will head over to the volunteer site." I looked at my watch and I saw the time. I responded, "You know it's 4 a.m., right?" He said, "Yea, so?" I wasn't sure if this was a test to see how interested I was in the organization, or if it was just an invitation. Whatever the reason, I said, "Irie see you at 6 a.m."

When I got to my room, I wondered why I agreed to get up at 6 in the morning to go to community service because I was so damn tired and just wanted to sleep in, I set my alarm, quickly fell asleep, and just as quickly was awoken by the sound of my alarm clock! I struggled to get out of bed but I did and walked over to the brothers' room. "Wow, you actually made it" he said, when he opened the door. We left campus and drove to an underprivileged area to paint a house. The house was part of a Habitat for Humanity build. When we started painting, I could tell everyone was still tired and were not in the mood to talk, but someone finally broke the ice and then we could not shut up! We were laughing, cracking jokes, sharing experiences, and connecting. After we were finished, representatives from Habitat for Humanity thanked us for our work and reminded us of the importance of it. We felt so accomplished serving and giving back to the community that we decided to treat ourselves to a hearty Denny's breakfast.

I mentioned earlier, going to the party was a fun social experience, but going to community service was a more rewarding one! I decided that I wanted to be part of that organization because of how much they valued service, and I was initiated that following spring. I share this story because even though I did not know it then, taking part in that community service project was the beginning of shaping me to become a Servant Leader. Servant Leadership is a term coined by Robert Greenleaf in which your goal as a leader is serving others. In serving others, you are giving people hope, a purpose, a path, someone who they can depend on, and giving back to those who at times might not have anything. This translates into service and giving back to the community which means so much to me. I always ask myself, *Am I doing enough? Can I do more? What am I not doing enough of? What areas can I give back to? Why am I not out there giving back more?* As a servant leader, I want to be sure that the people I am serving are getting the best version of me, and I am able to help them be the best versions of themselves.

Service was the final deciding factor for me to move forward to join my prestigious organization and for the organization to take a chance on me. Everyone always sees or talks about the parties that fraternities and sororities host, but no one sees when Greeks get up early in the morning to paint a house, feed the homeless, clean a road, etc. Why don't we promote our service projects more? Why don't we talk about the amount of hours we put in toward community service? Why don't we talk about the amount of money we fundraise for an organization? Why are we so scared to talk about service at all? Service is what makes your organizations stand out as positive, contributing, philanthropic members of the community. That community service project experience impacted me as a freshman, and I am sure there are projects out there that impact all of you as well.

Community service can do so much for your organization. For starters, it can promote and bring in new members that will bring value to your chapter. Service can also be a way for members in your organization to bond, and get to know one another. Yes, parties are fine and so are socials, but service is so special. This also gives members opportunities to grow personally, develop skills they might not have ever had before, and build memories that will last a lifetime. Community service projects can help when promoting your organization and in your new member recruitment efforts. Highlighting your organization's philanthropic involvements, promoting how many hours of community service hours completed— all of this will show you who is really interested in your organization. If service is something that does not mean anything to them, maybe that is an individual you should not extend a bid to or bring through your intake process. Or if you decided to take a chance on someone, maybe introducing that new member to service can change their lives forever.

If you are wondering about ways your organization can learn more about and get involved with community service opportunities, you may want to explore campus resources. Have you tried contacting your Civic Engagement office to see what opportunities are available? The Civic Engagement office always has opportunities and is looking for volunteers. Reach out to your National Headquarters to get more information about direct contacts for different organizations or even the national philanthropies your organization supports. Finally, there are more than likely several service organizations at your campus. Inquire about what opportunities they have and collaborate with them. Doing that will build relationships and provide even more opportunities.

If your organization takes pride in community service, then show it, live it, love it! Service should be an important factor of your organization, and it should be promoted just as much as you promote your socials and educational programs. Think about it, you are getting to know your brothers and sisters more and you are helping others in need while making a difference in the community. There is no better feeling than that. Don't believe me? Then go out, try it, and see for yourself. I dare you!

Tricia Benitez: Be the Change You Need

I remember being in second grade at Ella Dolhonde Elementary School, Mrs. Tranchant was my teacher. At the time I was fairly new and I always wanted to try to play basketball. I remember being at recess with these girls who, in my opinion, were basically the female young Michael Jordans of the second grade. The coach told them to include me, yet all that was included was the constant bullying and teasing from the other girls. As any normal eight-year-old, I immediately just sat on the ground and started crying and they played around me. Then I looked up at them and I asked

"Why can't we just all be friends and play together?" *Queue the mean girl laughter.*

The PE coach who was on duty that day whispered to my teacher and said that was one of the smartest things he had ever heard. Later that week I will never forget what my teacher Mrs. Tranchant told me: "Never let someone who doesn't see the goodness of your heart make you mean and cold. You are better than that. Never stop being a nice person."

I wanted to share that brief story with all of you in such a critical time of your lives of transitioning either from high school, no school, or even adulthood into college—especially if you're transitioning into a sorority or fraternity. I'm going to give you a series of exercises that you can take to your chapter as well as into life that will help cultivate the culture that you truly want. Go ahead and give yourself the permission to be the change that you needed when you first started. I promise your future self will thank you for it!

Something that you are definitely going to find—whether it's in your chapter and/or later in life—is that you may know somebody and be completely unaware you share the same pastimes and hobbies. If you want to go hiking, go ahead and put it out there that you want to go hiking. The plethora of ideas to do are never ending.

If you see someone struggling with their academics and you excel at that specific topic, go ahead and offer a Tuesday night tutor session and anyone can join. If you're an outdoor kind of person and you don't know who to do "outdoorsy" things with, there are so many platforms where you can make a post and create an event and have people show up. Even if it's just you and one other person, that's still a win!!

Who doesn't love to eat?!?! How cool would it be if on a Friday night your sorority put on a family dinner? What do I mean by that? I'm so glad you asked . . . essentially, it would be a budget-friendly potluck. This is also a great way to launch another event, especially if you go to one of your Friday night family dinners with your chapter and someone made a dish that is just delicious. Go ahead and ask them if they wouldn't mind doing a little mock cooking class to teach you their secret. Another little spin-off could be your chapter has a bake sale. Obviously get this approved by your higher education personnel. This is also a good way to get some funding for your chapter.

Maybe yoga is your thing. You don't have to have 500-hour yoga master credentials to participate in yoga or to love it. The best part about yoga is it literally can be free! If you were great at yoga, go ahead and offer a free yoga class that is at a public park and just put a little disclaimer that "hey it's free and donations are appreciated." You'll be so surprised how many people will happily contribute even if it's only a dollar.

The only time anyone should ever look down on somebody is when they are giving them a hand up. Be very conscious of others' feelings and make sure you're not participating in gossip. How would you feel if you were the one being talked about or put down? Change the subject or remove yourself from that dog-eat-dog circle.

Every morning for a month, write down three things that you're grateful for and three goals. For example:

1. I am grateful I got a good amount of sleep.
2. I am grateful I woke up and had an extremely sweet text from my boyfriend.
3. I am grateful I get to go to the gym today.

Trust me, some days these are not as easy as you would think. If you actually focus on three things at a minimum that you're grateful for as soon as you wake up, you live much happier more cohesive lives.

Writing down three goals can be the beginning of a positive, actionable plan. For example:

1. I am going to walk 10,000 steps today. I will take the stairs rather than the elevator. If I'm driving, I will park farther away from the door than I truly need to and I'll have this completed by 3 p.m.
2. I am going to read, or in my case listen to, some more of my book. I will not answer any text messages or social media notifications and I will also give myself an hour to read or listen to as much as I can within that hour uninterrupted.
3. I am going to go out of my way to befriend someone I do not know well. I will call them by their name and give them a genuine compliment as well as offer to open the door for them (or some other random act of kindness *and not post it*).

The 21/90 Rule says it takes 21 days to create a habit and 90 days to create a lifestyle.[60] But you have to purposefully make a conscious effort every single day. Not only will you be happier, but before you know it you will literally have changed the paradigm of the future!

I'm proud of you for reading this chapter as well as putting some of these tools to real-time use. Remember greatness is contagious. There are no glass ceilings and you can literally achieve anything you want in life as long as you put an intentional effort toward it daily.

---

[60] Claire O'Brien, "The 21/90 Rule: Make Life Better," Activeiron. com, January 10, 2020, https://www.activeiron.com/blog/ the-21-90-rule-make-life-better/.

Cassie Firebaugh joins us from Indianapolis, Indiana, and this former NFL cheerleader (Go Colts!) is no stranger to the challenges the game of life throws her way. As a busy mom of six, business owner, and entrepreneur, it's safe to say she definitely has a few balls of her own to keep in the air!

However, that very full life came to a screeching halt one evening as she experienced a stroke on her birthday that changed everything. Against the odds, two weeks later she had a second one. Cassie has tackled many obstacles such as living with a heart defect, single motherhood, and multiple business creation and ownership. Today as her story continues, she is living proof that you can turn pain and fear into power and fuel. Cassie is passionate about using her voice to inspire students to confidently stand up and use their own to speak to be heard.

Her love for all things Greek is deeply rooted in her time at Indiana University-Bloomington where she was a member of the Beta chapter of Pi Beta Phi. Cassie also has served as a Panhellenic representative and is beyond excited to continue this journey. She not only engages students with her humor and heart, but offers impactful programs for the development of empowered leaders throughout campus and beyond.

You can see Cassie's presentations at: www.greekuniversity. org/cassie

Email: cassie@greekuniversity.org

When you see Edson O'Neale walk into a room, your first perception might be that he is a strong, confident, empowered man, but there's more to Edson than meets the eye. His stature may seem imposing to you, but he has felt small. His voice is clear as a bell, but he's often felt unheard. He is very present, but he has been made to feel invisible. Yet through it all, he's tried his best to *be* his best.

He's overcome what he's felt. He's reshaped his narrative.

The why, the how, and the way, he shares in his talks about leadership, bullying, and history. Compelled to rewrite your story and change perceptions? Work with Edson today and discover:

1. Dynamic thought leader focused on values and self-worth
2. Your supportive accountability partner for achieving future goals
3. A champion of consistent growth

As a college student, Edson was an outstanding leader involved in Student Government, Campus Activities, Student Organizations, and of course Greek Life. Edson crossed the burning sands of the Rho Xi chapter of Alpha Phi Alpha Fraternity, Inc. in the spring of 2004 and never looked back. He served in several roles such as Secretary Community Service Chair, Educational Chair, Vice President, and ultimately chapter President—their organization won Fraternity of the Year under his leadership. Edson graduated with a degree in Sport Management from Saint Leo University in December of 2007. He furthered his education in 2009 when he became a Graduate Assistant at Nova Southeastern University in programming. Working there, he realized his passion for working with students. He graduated with a Master of Science Degree in Leadership in December of 2010.

You can see Edson's presentations at:
www.greekuniversity.org/edson

Email: edson@greekuniversity.org

Tricia Benitez and her family were no strangers to addiction. Her father suffered from alcoholism, her mother admits to doing cocaine on several occasions, and her brother struggled for a long time with drugs. These active addictions were also noticed by the authorities. Tricia's mother left her when she was an infant, trying to give her away like a puppy to a distant family in Florida. Tricia's father had an addiction that resulted in Tricia being taken away by the state as a child. Orphanage was the child's version of a jail. Tricia was fortunate to have a sister who was eighteen years older, and she had the ability to get Tricia out of the orphanage. Her sister played such an instrumental part of her life by helping to raise Tricia, as well as continuously being supportive of her career in the midst of a very dysfunctional family. Tricia's brother lost his battle from addiction, going in and out of treatment centers numerous times himself. On June 8, 2002, his landlord found him dead in his apartment due to a drug overdose.

Tricia's dad demonstrated how to live a gypsy life, so she found it "normal" to shack up with lots of people. In her early twenties, she found herself in a horrible relationship. Tricia ran away and turned to meth to escape. When she finally escaped, it was with a gun to her head, $100 to her name, four bags of clothes, and her dog named Pink.

Tricia has completely turned her life around since that day. Much of her time has been spent as a Treatment Specialist for Addiction Campuses in Nashville, Tennessee. There, she was on the front lines of the opioid epidemic and other forms of addiction as a resource for people to get help instead of landing in jail or worse. Tricia has helped almost 1,500 people get the help and treatment they need for their addictions over the last six years. Tricia shares her own powerful story of addiction and dysfunctional relationships with students all across the country to ensure that they get the help they need for themselves or others on their campus, as well as showing the students what a healthy relationship should look like.

You can see Tricia's presentations at:
www.greekuniversity.org/tricia

Email: tricia@greekuniversity.org

CHAPTER 10

A United Front: Collaboration between Student Organizations and Campus Leaders

Michael Ayalon

O ne of the most critical relationships that new members must start to develop is the relationship between their organization and the administration. Yes, it is a shared responsibility, but as a student, those relationships have helped me and my organization tremendously, so it makes sense for you to actively pursue them and start that process now. It was these relationships that allowed my fraternity chapter to do significant fundraising in the community in the form of working security at concerts that came to the University at Buffalo (including Public Enemy, Gin Blossoms, Better Than Ezra, and Cypress Hill), as well as working the concession stands at the major sporting events in town for the NHL (Sabres) and the NFL (Bills). I would have never even known about these opportunities without the connections I had with campus administrators. Our chapter had all kinds of things we wanted to buy (composites, a new sound/light system, a foosball table, and a dart machine), but we somehow felt limited in the ways we could do fundraising as a group. Thank goodness the administration had some great ways for us to earn some additional money.

These relationships started when my chapter president took me to the Fraternity and Sorority Life (FSL) office and introduced me to our campus advisor. Whenever I walked by that office, I was sure to stop by and say hi for no reason at all. If I was having a problem, I wanted them to be aware so I could get their advice. They had a window into some of the things we were working on as a chapter. You should try to connect with the FSL office at least once a week. You might even think about dropping off some donuts or coffee every once in a while too, because they typically work long hours and sometimes forget to take a break. Those relationships that I developed in the Fraternity and Sorority Life office were not only important to me while I was in college, but they are still very important to me today as I consider them my mentors and also close friends.

Why else was that relationship important with the administration? It allowed me to get resources for my chapter in the areas where we needed help, such as tutors and financial aid for brothers who were struggling. You might be wondering, shouldn't the relationship between the administration and student organizations just come naturally?

Why do we sometimes see a gap between fraternities/ sororities and campus leaders? Aren't these organizations and the university completely aligned?

The national Gallup-Purdue Index study of 30,000 college graduates showed that fraternity and sorority members showed higher workplace engagement, are thriving in five elements of well-being, have higher alumni attachment, and felt more prepared for life after college.[61] So, why aren't the relationships closer between these two entities since we are ultimately working toward the same goals?

Think about your experience as a high school student. You developed test-taking abilities for the standardized tests (SAT, ACT, or AP exams, for example). But did you have a shared learning experience with your teachers where they learned alongside you? The administrators on college campuses have spent years in masters programs and many have gone through doctoral programs as well, but that has created a distance between undergraduate students and the administration. How can the students see the administrators as real people? Are they accessible outside of class, or are they doing additional research with their time? If we truly want a great college experience, then we must focus on these critical relationships that are based on human interaction. Those close relationships gave me more motivation to succeed in college, more resilience, more problem-solving skills, more satisfaction in the experience, and it made me a loyal alumnus who continues to give back to his alma mater.

---

[61] "Fraternities and Sororities: Understanding Life Outcomes," May 27, 2014, https://www.gallup.com/services/176279/fraternities-sororities-understanding-life-outcomes.aspx.

Friendship is an overused word. We could meet someone in passing and introduce them as "my friend Alex" to another person. There are many different levels to a friendship, just as there are many different levels of interaction between college students and campus leaders. As students, we can move from a general student to a mentoring relationship with a college professor by doing various things. Perhaps we can sit in the front row of class, we can attend the professor's office hours, we can raise our hand in class and actively participate, and maybe we can even volunteer for a common cause in our community with a professor outside of the classroom. The more activities that we share, the closer we can get to a shared learning experience and a mentoring relationship that could last a lifetime.

It's not all about the students, it's also about the administration. Administrators, staff, and professors want to feel engaged at work too! Believe it or not, the administration wants to be teaching and learning, otherwise they wouldn't be working on a college campus. *Retention* is another big buzz word on college campuses. They want to understand your needs and provide you with the tools you need to be successful. But how can they understand your needs without the frequency of interaction? Collaboration is essential for their success and your success.

In order to build true collaboration between student organizations and the administration, there are four steps involved in the process. Let's take alcohol/drug abuse on college campuses as a problem we want to solve:

- Step # 1, students need to be able to share their opinions and ideas. Students might believe that more could be done to educate about the dangers of alcohol/drug abuse and build bystander intervention skills among those in the community.

- Step # 2, opportunities should be given to the students to become more involved. So, perhaps students can bring in a speaker to address the student body about building a community of care, changing the stereotypes of fraternity/sorority life, and practical harm reduction strategies at our social events.

- Step # 3, students will take an active role. So, perhaps students will get TIPS (Training for Intervention ProcedureS) certified on intervention procedures to help when they see a student who has too much to drink at a social event. Or perhaps students will collectively sign up for yoga classes, healthy eating classes, or get involved in sports on campus to help manage their stress without using drugs or alcohol.

- Step # 4, students and the administration have joint ownership of the process. For example, perhaps the students and the administration develop a medical amnesty policy where you can call and get campus police involved to help save someone's life without fear of getting in trouble for possession of alcohol or drugs. This is what true collaboration could look like, and it can be applied to just about any problem that you're trying to solve on a college campus.

At the University of Alabama, the campus community developed an initiative called "Out 2 Lunch." Any student can invite an administrator out for lunch or coffee on campus at a dining facility to enjoy some food together and have a conversation. Even if the two parties have completely different viewpoints, good food is usually something we can all agree on. In this case, the student actually pays for the administrator's meal. They have a conversation about improving some part of campus life. Afterward, the student fills out an assessment on why they chose this administrator, what they learned, and how satisfied they were with the conversation that took place. Once the assessment is submitted to the university, the dining facility will issue a credit back to the student for the money used to cover the administrator's meal. Could you establish a similar program on your campus? Think about the connections that could be made with such a program and the problems that could be solved together.

Could you have monthly conversations with administrators as a group? Could you invite an equal amount of students and administrators to attend an event with round tables to brainstorm ideas on ways to improve your campus for a specified amount of time? The key to this experiment working is to be respectful at all times and to listen to the various opinions presented, even if you happen to disagree with that opinion. Each table could be a different topic, and students/ administrators could be randomly moved around to different topics and different tables. In order to get the conversation started, perhaps each student and administrator could read a news story about something happening on campus and how you could work together to address this issue. You must have good listening skills to hear the other person's perspectives if this is going to work! Then document the experience for each person (both the students and the administrator) who participates with an assessment and encourage feedback for the same event next month.

Why are these conversations between students and administrators so important? You may meet an administrator that you don't talk to often. Perhaps this meeting could be the start of a mentoring relationship. It's also possible that you could solve some really difficult problems together. Most of all, you will feel that you are an active participant in making your community better and that you are both heard. You'll now see the administrators as real people whom you can approach with problems and potential solutions for those problems. As you begin to see the shared responsibility in building a better campus community, you'll slowly start to see the improvements you've been looking for.

Another way to collaborate with the administration is to bring them closer to you. Have you thought about alumni initiations into your fraternity or sorority for administrators on campus that are not already members of the fraternity/ sorority community? Yes, alumni are initiated into your fraternity or sorority all the time. It's a way of recognizing them. Don't we need more people fighting our fight from the inside? I would highly suggest this strategy when you are working with someone in the administration who goes above and beyond to help your organization. They will feel very appreciative you want them to be a part of your organization and become a fully initiated member, they will better understand your values and needs, and now they will join you as an affiliated member. Imagine if the entire administration was affiliated with a fraternity or sorority on campus, and how that would change some of the conversations and frustrations that you have currently. Contact your fraternity/sorority headquarters on how you can do an alumni initiation for a member of the administration on your campus.

You're already doing community service in your organization. Don't you need some more hands? Invite the administration, staff, and faculty to do community service with your organization on a regular basis. There's something about doing community service that brings people closer together. When you're serving food to the hungry in your community and you're standing shoulder to shoulder with someone from the administration, I promise that both of you will leave not only feeling as if you've made a difference in your community, but also with a greater appreciation for each other. Don't forget to take photos and document the event by writing up a summary of the event and sharing those photos with the local and school newspaper. It shows your organization in a great light, and that the administration is working with you to tackle these problems in your community. Suddenly your professors and other students who are not affiliated will want to join you in your mission, and those stereotypes about Fraternity and Sorority Life will begin to evaporate.

Wouldn't you love to have quality new members in your organization? Of course! Send a letter to the administration, professors, and faculty of your institution outlining who your organization is, what your values are, the types of community service you are regularly involved with, and the type of student your organization is looking for. Add your name, phone number, and email address and ask that the administration contact you if they know of a student who would make an excellent addition to your organization. By engaging the administration in the recruitment process, you have now made them a partner and advocate for your organization. They are much more likely to support your organization because they helped to recruit the members inside, and now you have a new source of leads for students to join your organization. This is a win-win.

Could you work alongside the administration to grow your organization? Think about all the job opportunities that are available in residence life, admissions, freshman orientation, and campus tours. Students need to lead in these areas on behalf of the university to help grow the campus, and they are looking for outgoing students that know how to socialize. This is the perfect opportunity for fraternity and sorority members to form new relationships with campus administrators, make some additional income as a part-time job, and meet new students that are coming on campus who are looking to get involved in organizations. It's mutually beneficial. If you aren't already involved in these areas on campus, you're missing out on a great opportunity to build positive relationships with other students and the administration.

Finally, do what you say you're going to do. As fraternity and sorority members, we don't like it when the media reports on all the bad things that our organizations do, instead of reporting on all the money that we raise for our national philanthropy or our community service work. The media is reporting on the inconsistencies. If your organization states that you're all about scholarship in your creed/motto, then your chapter GPA should be higher than the average student GPA on campus. If your organization talks about service in your creed/motto, then your fraternity or sorority calendar shouldn't be 95 percent social events. There should be a healthy balance between service events and social events. What is your chapter's four-year graduation rate, and how does that compare with the four-year graduation rate on campus for all students? What is your chapter's retention rate, and how does that compare with the university's retention rate? These are the types of metrics that you want to get familiar with and have discussions with the administration on which ones are very good, and which ones that you might need some help in improving. We must do what we say we are going to do as an organization, otherwise the media will call us out and it creates more distance between our organization and the administration.

The sense of belonging is a critical piece of college satisfaction. Yes, joining a student organization certainly helps with belonging. However, your relationships and interaction with the administration also contributes to your sense of belonging and overall satisfaction with your overall university experience. I hope that you will take full advantage of these relationships with campus leaders and find the lifetime of rewards that comes with those relationships. I have found it, and I'm better because of it.

Michael Ayalon is a professional speaker, author, host of the Fraternity Foodie Podcast, and CEO of Greek University. He has headlined keynote presentations on over 200 college campuses in 35 states to help solve problems such as Sexual Assault, Hazing, Alcohol and Drug Abuse, and recruitment for college student organizations. As a speaker, he is able to take lessons learned from helping to build companies from startup to over $25 million in annual sales, as well as best practices as the Former Executive Director of Sigma Pi Fraternity with 120 chapters and over 100,000 members, to create dynamic, positive, and results-driven keynotes and workshops that transform people's lives.

Mike is a graduate of the School of Management at the University at Buffalo, and has a Master's Degree from Cumberland University in Public Service Management.

You can see Mike's presentations at www.greekuniversity. org/presentations

Email Mike: bookings@greekuniversity.org

CHAPTER 11

The Effects of Membership Recruitment/Intake on Chapter Culture

By: Dr. Ed Dadez and Edson O'Neale

Membership recruitment is important because of each specific Greek fraternity and sorority Ritual. The Ritual is sacred and only those who are worthy of moving forward will experience the Ritual. When going through membership recruitment, it gives the brothers and sisters of the organization a perspective of who they are bringing into their respective chapter and gives the interested gentleman/woman a look at what chapter he or she is seeking membership.

Not only is recruitment important, but both parties should take this process very seriously. You are not just joining a

Greek organization; you are joining a prestigious brotherhood and sisterhood that will last a lifetime. The Ritual and the intake process bounds you for life and that is why it is so important to consider the magnitude of this decision. This is where miscommunications sometimes occur. There is more of a focus on increasing membership numbers which may harm the chapter rather than understanding the importance of choosing men and women who believe in what the chapter is about. Membership intake and new member education are about personal development, support, and professionalism. The founders of our fraternities and sororities did not create them to haze members. They started these organizations to provide opportunities and a space for men and women to evolve into someone special who will live the Ritual for life. We must always remember what our founders sacrificed for and continue the legacy they started.

After membership recruitment and/or rush, then membership intake and/or new member education become center stage. Potential candidates and/or new members must fully understand the process. Many Greek advisors and chapter advisors have heard individuals say, "When I went through my recruitment process, I was sold on a dream and when I accepted my bid and joined my respective organization, it was completely different." Fraternity and sorority members need to understand you cannot be fake and pretend to be someone you are not. By doing that you are not representing your organization well and outlining the values and ethics of the organization. If you as a current member are not representing the organization in the way it should be, how can you expect new members to do the same? When fraternity and sorority members are meeting potential candidates for the first time, be very transparent and honest. Obviously, there is certain information as current members you cannot share, but be as transparent about the values, the culture, and what type of person you are looking for to join your organization. As you seek new members, ask interested candidates:

- Do you see yourself being an active member of this chapter?
- What are your values?
- What are you looking for when it comes to joining a chapter?
- What do you have to offer our chapter?
- Why is our chapter the best choice for you?
- How do you see yourself as a leader?
- What activities are you involved in on campus?

These are the types of conversations you should be having—not telling them things that have no value to you, to them, or even the Greek chapter. Remember you are looking for quality members to enhance your organization and to make it stronger so you can make a difference in the community.

Effective member recruitment, rush, new member intake, and pledging will lead to the development of positive and successful chapters, members, and a culture that will make a difference in the lives of all those who choose to join a brotherhood or sisterhood. The following Cs are needed to accomplish this goal:

- **Camaraderie:** Greek organizations are about brotherhood or sisterhood. The fellowship and friendships that are made will last forever.

Choosing to join an organization is an important decision that will assist members throughout their lives.

- **Caring:** Greek members need to care about themselves, each other, their chapter, Greek system, and lastly their college. Caring will ensure that chapter members will make the right decisions based on their Ritual, values, and ethics.

- **Celebration:** It is important that every Greek organization find times to celebrate the victories. This will assist in the bonding of the membership and improve the overall community of the chapter as well as the Greek system.

- **Challenge:** Fraternities and sororities will face challenges throughout the year. The membership will be strengthened as they deal with adversity. Dealing with conflict effectively will assist all members and the organization to move forward invigorated to continue to improve and develop into a successful chapter.

- **Change:** Once you think everything is perfect, something will happen. Change is inevitable. Greek organizations need to be prepared for the unexpected. Contingency plans are always important to have.

- **Character:** Every Greek member needs to realize that their thoughts, behaviors, actions, motives, and habits directly relate to personal integrity and morality. Reciting and living our Ritual should mean to each of us that we have agreed to be men and women of character. If we cannot do this, we should not be members of a fraternity or sorority.

- **Collaboration:** The ability to work together in and outside of the organization is crucial. There must be cooperation and teamwork which will greatly assist the organization and members to be successful.

- **Commitment:** When we choose to join a Greek chapter, we have agreed to be committed to our organizational ritual, values, and ethics. We need to be firm with our members and fellow Greek organizations to live the ritualistic values that we have sworn to abide by.

- **Communication:** There is a substantial need for there to be clear communication at all levels of the chapter as well with the Greek Council, alumni corporation, university, and national organization. At times both written and verbal communication may be necessary and helpful. This will ensure that every Greek member hears the same message.

- **Community:** The purpose of membership recruitment, member intake, and new member education should always be to strengthen fraternities and sororities. If we focus on this purpose, we will see our Greek chapters thrive and prosper which will ensure that our Greek communities will be respected and trusted.

- **Confidence:** Greek members and chapters must have the confidence to believe in themselves and just as importantly their Ritual, values, and ethics. Confidence, not arrogance will assist all members and chapters to live their values and be proud to share who they are and what they stand for as brothers and sisters.

- **Courage:** As we all know it takes individual courage to stand up in front of your brothers and sisters to say and/or do the right thing. Too often, our members may choose to follow the crowd rather than to confront the brutal facts and follow the guidelines from our chapter values and ethics. We must do a better job of confronting those who choose act or behave in a way that is counter to what we are about.

There are many key relationships that are vital for continued growth and development of the fraternity/sorority as well as its membership:

- The relationship between each member and the brotherhood/sisterhood needs to be one of trust, respect, and honor. Each member must feel that s/he has worth and is appreciated by the organization.
- The relationship between the officers and the membership is one that is paramount. The officers must be clear in not only "walking the walk" but "talking the talk" as it applies to the true meaning of being a brother or sister of the chapter. All must strive to ensure that this is clearly understood.
- The relationship between the classes is necessary for there to be continuity and continued progress. Too often it is the junior class in charge of the chapter hoping that the seniors who were once leaders not

make it tough for them by acting inappropriately. Former chapter officers must become mentors for the next set of officers, not combatants as it pertains to policies, procedures, and processes. Additionally, new members who tend to be first year must never be disrespected or hazed by any of the other chapter classes. This is against every chapter, university, and national organization policy as well as against the law. It is imperative that this behavior is dealt with as quickly as possible.

- The relationship with the respective Greek Council may not seem as important, but it is one that is very significant. This is the organization that should remind each chapter to live up to their oaths and rituals. A clear vision, mission, and mutual goals should be developed to strengthen Greek Life throughout the college or university.

- The relationship with alumni members can sometimes be one of the most difficult to handle. Those alumni who do not live up to their Ritual and then return to relive the "good old days" can cause irreparable harm to the chapter. Alumni corporations must be actively involved ensuring that these alumni members are dealt with swiftly. It cannot be left to the undergraduate members to handle these situations by themselves.

- The relationship with the Alumni (House) Corporation is critical. These organizations must see the relationship as one where the corporation "lends" the charter to the chapter leadership and chapter each year. The Alumni Corporations need to understand that if the current membership causes harm to their relationship with the university and/ or National Organization and the charter is lost, it may not come back to the corporation. It may be lost forever. The alumni must ensure that they are teaching the current brotherhood/sisterhood what it means to be a member of their organization.

- The relationship with the National Organization is one that needs to be mutually beneficial for both the undergraduate chapter and the alumni corporation. These three groups together should strive to develop strong GLOs on every college and university campus. The National working with the alumni and undergraduate chapter must continue to ensure the Ritual, values, and ethics of the group are understood and lived by daily by all members. A critical component of this relationship is the annual or biannual visit by a member of the national organization. This opportunity should be seen as a prime time to assess the effectiveness of the chapter and to view how it matches up with other chapters.

Would you join an organization that does not match your values? Would you want someone to be a part of your organization that could diminish or destroy your chapter? We don't think so. As we conclude this chapter, take the time to evaluate your chapter's values and ask, Are we upholding the values of our organization? Then look in the mirror and ask yourself:

- Am *I* upholding the values of my organization?

- Am I upholding my own values as a person?
- Is this something ten years, twenty years, thirty years down the road, I will look back on and reminisce about?
- Or will I look back at my experience in college and regret my time with my organization?

Be that one that stands out—be the trendsetter, ask the questions, and start the conversations. The whole point of this chapter is to open your eyes and take a long hard look at yourself and your chapter. Unfortunately, there are people who do not support Greek Life and they would love to see it no longer exist. Are you going to be the one to give in to those people, or are you going to rise above to be the example you are meant to be? As you are reading this, you might be saying to yourself that you have nothing to prove to haters. *Why should I focus my energy on them?* You are not wrong, but you CAN have a positive, "go-getter" mindset within yourself and your chapters that may help dispel the haters.

Be the Letters—do not let the Letters be you. Live the dream, set the foundation, and make a difference!

After a successful thirty-nine-year career in university administration in student affairs and continuing education at Ohio State University, University of Dayton, Michigan State University, Bucknell University, Chowan University, and Saint Leo University, Dr. Ed Dadez shifted his full-time focus to the classroom. He is a Visiting Professor in the department of graduate education. His professional interests are in higher education leadership; history and philosophy of higher education; campus ecology; and student affairs administration. He has presented at numerous local, state, regional, and international conferences as well as written in a number of different publications.

Previous to transitioning to academic affairs, Dr. Ed Dadez was named Vice President of Student Affairs in March 2000. Over eighteen years, he led and supervised thirteen student affairs and campus operations departments. Along with the student affairs division for eleven years, he also led and supervised 40+ education centers and the online program.

Email Dr. Dadez: ed.dadez@saintleo.edu

When you see Edson O'Neale walk into a room, your first perception might be that he is a strong, confident, empowered man, but there's more to Edson than meets the eye. His stature may seem imposing to you, but he has felt small. His voice is clear as a bell, but he's often felt unheard. He is very present, but he has been made to feel invisible. Yet through it all, he's tried his best to *be* his best.

He's overcome what he's felt. He's reshaped his narrative.

The why, the how, and the way, he shares in his talks about leadership, bullying, and history. Compelled to rewrite your story and change perceptions? Work with Edson today and discover:

1. Dynamic thought leader focused on values and self-worth.
2. Your supportive accountability partner for achieving future goals.
3. A champion of consistent growth.

As a college student, Edson was an outstanding leader involved in Student Government, Campus Activities, Student Organizations, and of course Greek Life. Edson crossed the burning sands of the Rho Xi chapter of Alpha Phi Alpha Fraternity, Inc. in the spring of 2004 and never looked back. He served in several roles such as Secretary Community Service Chair, Educational Chair, Vice President, and ultimately chapter President—their organization won Fraternity of the Year under his leadership. Edson graduated with a degree in Sport Management from Saint Leo University in December of 2007. He furthered his education in 2009 when he became a Graduate Assistant at Nova Southeastern University in programming. Working there, he realized his passion for working with students. He graduated with a Master of Science Degree in Leadership in December of 2010.

You can see Edson's presentations at: www.greekuniversity.org/edson

Email: edson@greekuniversity.org

CHAPTER 12

Networking Opportunities during New Member Education and Beyond

Michael Ayalon

O ne of the biggest benefits you have as a new member of your fraternity or sorority is the network that you now belong to. While you might only see your chapter brothers or sisters, you belong to one of the largest networking organizations on the planet—and it's called Fraternity and Sorority Life. If you belong to a national or international organization, you may have well over 100,000 members in your organization. Even if you belong to a local organization, you are now a member of the fraternity and sorority community, and that means something to members of other organizations that went through similar experiences running committees or serving on their local executive board.

You belong to a movement much larger than yourself, and to take advantage of these resources, you'll need to understand how to network.

Have you asked yourself why you're in college? Yes, you want to make the world a better place. However, you're also spending lots of money to attend your university. You're making that exchange because you believe that you're going to have a good job with that degree framed on the wall behind you. You should be saying hi to everyone on campus and starting meaningful conversations with them, because the larger your network, the more opportunities you'll have at graduation and during your career.

The first thing you need to do is to develop an ease in talking about what you do best and what opportunities you're looking for. Everyone reading this book has a talent and a passion that can translate to success beyond the walls of your campus, but if you don't develop an ease in talking about those things, who is going to know about it? Networking can be defined as the deliberate process of exchanging information, resources, support, and access to create mutually beneficial relationships for personal and professional success. Notice the words "mutually beneficial relationships." It's not all about you. Instead, it's about helping each other reach your goals. You can absolutely start this process while you're in college.

One of my favorite networking stories is when Mayor Cory Booker (before he ran for President and before he became a US Senator of New Jersey) went to a dinner at a conference in Idaho in July of 2010. Mayor Booker was seated at the same table as the founder of Facebook, Mark Zuckerberg. Mayor Booker talked about the problems with the school system in Newark, New Jersey. After that conversation, in September of 2010, Mark Zuckerberg made an announcement that he was donating $100 million of his personal fortune to the Newark school system. Zuckerberg had absolutely no known ties to Newark at that time, but because of a networking opportunity, Mayor Booker got the funding he so desperately needed. Neither one of them attended the dinner conference in Idaho thinking that this would be the outcome. It was a conversation about needs in the community, and how they could work together to solve this problem. The lesson here is to always attend that dinner, go to the conference, and meet as many people as you can. You never know how that chance meeting could turn into an internship, a job, a new career, a new entrepreneurial venture, a new product, or a new service.

Networking is a long-term process. You can't microwave a relationship for thirty seconds. However, you can start now while you're in college. The process can start in your chapter by letting your other members know what you do well and what opportunities you are looking for. You shouldn't start the process when you absolutely need a job at graduation. By then, all the good jobs are taken, and you've missed out on great opportunities. Your job is to build top-of-the-mind awareness about what you do well so that your chapter members and others in the community think of you when an opportunity pops up. For example, if you're really good at social media and you have a slick Instagram account that is well branded, you want others in your chapter and others in the fraternity/sorority community to know this is one of your skills and that you're willing to help out. Perhaps you can help to customize the chapter Instagram account. Perhaps you can build an Instagram account for your council to attract more new members into your fraternity/sorority community. If you do these things, show your skills, and build that awareness, it will lead to internships and jobs in the future when everyone in your chapter and community brings these opportunities directly to you. The key is to build REAL, human connections. Handing out business cards is not networking. Proving that you do something really well, showing that you're willing to help out, and building top-of-the-mind awareness about your skills in your community is networking.

I have built some really strong connections within the fraternity/sorority advisors, and they know that I bring strong educational programs on topics such as hazing prevention, sexual assault prevention, and alcohol/drug abuse prevention. I have a few advisors that recommend me to everyone they know, and I get lots of referrals from them because they know I will expertly serve their peers/coworkers. They know I will arrive early, give multiple programs to multiple audiences, delight their students, and bring real positive change to their communities in the form of a safer campus. These referrals from these advisors brings in more new business than all of our marketing efforts combined. Don't underestimate the value of networking referral generation. Think about the most successful people you know. They have built a network and have mastered the art and science of networking. Business just flows to them.

I encourage you to attend alumni events and your fraternity/sorority conferences and conventions. When you meet an alumnus of your chapter, or an alumnus of your fraternity/ sorority, there will be three questions that will come up in that encounter:

1. Who are you?
2. What do you do?
3. What are we going to talk about now?

You must have answers already developed to these questions. For the last question, have a success story ready to go. Think about a time in your college career where you had a big victory. Perhaps you helped to recruit the largest new member class on campus. Perhaps you increased your chapter GPA from 2.6 to 3.2, and it was the highest chapter GPA on campus. How did you accomplish this goal? Have this success story ready in your mind so you can share that with this alumnus, and ultimately they will figure out how this story applies to their business or their network, and how you might be able to help them.

Have you developed your USP yet? Your USP is a Unique Selling Proposition. Start with twelve words that you have memorized and ready to roll off your tongue. As you get more experience with it, you can expand those twelve words. You need to deliver your USP to people in networking situations. Here's mine: *"I empower college students to create safer communities, and help them attract more quality new members than they can possibly handle."* If someone asks me what I do for a living, doesn't that sound better than "I'm a speaker on college campuses"? When you develop your USP, here is the structure: "I help [target market] [solve problem]." Write down your own USP on a piece of paper now.

Don't forget people's names. If you're like me and you tend to forget names, be sure to repeat their name when you meet them. Say, "It's nice to meet you, Robert." Try to introduce that person to at least one other person at the event, and through the introduction, it will help you to remember that person's name and retain it. When you say your name, you can separate and articulate that name. "I'm Mike, Mike Ayalon." If your last name is hard to spell like mine is, try to make your name memorable. "It's like Avalon but with a Y." Now you've memorized my name.

If you're in a situation where you meet a whole bunch of alumni or people at the same time, it can be hard to remember everyone's name. Be friendly, say hi, and then go back to each person individually and introduce yourself one-on-one using the system in the paragraph above. It will work! Even if you forget someone's name, you can say something like, "I remember you, I'm Mike." The other person will most likely say their name back to you. You can also make some comments about the conversation you had with them before. Then say, "Tell me your name again?" Alternatively, you can always find someone in the room who knows everyone and they can remind you about their name. Use their name often, it's their favorite word in their vocabulary.

If you find yourself in a networking situation and you're talking to a business owner or hiring manager, ask questions!

- How long have you been in this business?
- Why did you start the business?
- Who are your customers?
- Where is the business located?

- Do you serve customers locally only or all over the country?
- What is your biggest challenge right now?
- How can I help you?

If you can introduce them to someone else in the meeting that can help them, you should do it! Once you get answers to all of these questions, if that person who can help them is you, then now is the time to tell them how much you appreciated the meeting. Make sure you get their contact information and explain to them the next steps in working with you.

Now you might be wondering where you can meet all of these wonderful networking contacts as a college student. They are all around you! Obviously, you want to attend all of your fraternity conferences and conventions because there are many successful alumni who attend these events. Many national or international fraternities and sororities have membership directories where you can search for alumni by location or by industry. If you have a job or internship right now, be sure to attend their group outings after work and on the weekends as well. Your family and friends know people in your industry that they can introduce you to. There are networking organizations in every city in the country, just use Google and search for networking events in your city. Rotary clubs are a great place to meet community leaders, so be sure to stop by your local Rotary meeting to get introduced to these leaders. Meetup.com and Eventbrite. com are good websites to locate local events. Check in with the career service center at your University to find local events. Professional associations, chambers of commerce in your city, volunteer groups, athletics/hobbies, and religious organizations in your community are all great places to find community and business leaders to network with.

Give more than you receive at these events. If there is a bunch of bottled water that needs to be handed out to the attendees, start handing them out. If there are documents that need to be distributed to each person, pass out a sheet to everyone in attendance. You really want to act more like a host than a guest. Go with the mindset that you're going to be as helpful as you can be. Get to know the leaders of the event and ask them how you can help. Karma is real. I help as many people as I can, and good things just happen. The person I help might not be the person who helps me, but it's just the way the universe works. Be helpful and be kind.

Once you start meeting with people in your industry, be sure that you have a strategy to communicate with them following the event. You should get access to a CRM (customer relationship management) database online. Some of these are free and some have a low monthly cost depending on the features they provide. It will allow you to organize all your contacts, keep records on all the communications you have with them, and set follow-up calls/emails/meetings. For the people that can help you right now with an internship or job, send them an email within twenty-four hours of meeting them. It can be three sentences: 1) your name and where you met them, 2) the fact that you enjoyed meeting them, and 3) if they need your help, they should reach out to you.

While you're brushing up your résumé, be sure to also create a LinkedIn profile for yourself right now. Don't wait. Get a professional photo for your account, use keywords that relate to your career or field of study, and include all of your skills. Start building your network on LinkedIn from current and prior employers, your organization, and from your college/university. Get references added to your LinkedIn account from other people in your network. That will help when future employers are looking at your profile to build credibility. Join career-related groups or start your own if you can't find any good ones. Be sure to answer questions in these groups and ask questions too. You want to showcase your knowledge and be a resource for companies seeking your expertise. Once you've built up some connections on LinkedIn, don't be afraid to post about the types of opportunities you are looking for. In both your résumé and on your LinkedIn profile, be sure to add the positions you have held in your organization, and demonstrate to me with data how you made a difference. Don't just put treasurer. Tell me with numbers and statistics how you made a difference. For example, did you reduce chapter expenses by 30 percent? Did you increase chapter revenues by 25 percent through new community partnerships? Those are the things that should appear on your résumé and LinkedIn profile so we can have a conversation on how you did those things and how that relates to my company if I were to hire you.

As a college student, you will have tons of people that will say "If there's anything I can do to help you find a job or opportunity, let me know!" There are many things that person can do to assist you with an internship or job. They can display your products or services. They can make an announcement for you in online groups they are in. They can invite you to attend events with them. They can endorse your products/services online. They can nominate you for an award. They can make the initial contact for you with potential customers/prospects. They can arrange a meeting for you. They can publish information on your behalf on their website or blog. They can connect with you on LinkedIn. Don't be afraid to leverage your network to help you get to where you want to go—as long as you are also looking to help them in return.

Finally, write thank-you notes. In a world filled with text messages and emails, as a business owner, I notice when someone sends me a handwritten thank-you note in the mail. It stands out. As a college student, get in the habit of writing thank-you notes to the people you meet. The impression you will leave with them goes much further than an email. If you follow this plan all throughout your college career, you'll have so many great opportunities headed your way!

Michael Ayalon is a professional speaker, author, host of the *Fraternity Foodie Podcast*, and CEO of Greek University. He has headlined keynote presentations on over 200 college campuses in 35 states to help solve problems such as sexual assault, hazing, alcohol and drug abuse, and recruitment for college student organizations. As a speaker, he is able to take lessons learned from helping to build companies from startup to over $25 million in annual sales, as well as best practices as the Former Executive Director of Sigma Pi Fraternity with 120 chapters and over 100,000 members, to create dynamic, positive, and results-driven keynotes and workshops that transform people's lives.

Mike is a graduate of the School of Management at the University at Buffalo, and has a Master's Degree from Cumberland University in Public Service Management.

You can see Mike's presentations at:
www.greekuniversity.org/presentations

Email Mike: bookings@greekuniversity.org

CHAPTER 13

COVID, College, Drugs, and Drink:
Arming with the Shield of NO

Dr. Louis Profeta

I've never met a heroin addict that did not try heroin.

I've never met someone who has driven drunk that did not get drunk.

I've never taken care of a college student who died from drug or alcohol abuse that did not consume drugs or alcohol.

We have to address hazing on college campuses, there is no question. But the majority of college students don't haze or participate in hazing. They are, for the most part, good and honorable people who would never consider causing physical harm to another or coercing a friend to engage in dangerous behavior. But still, the start of each new year will bring with it new headlines and videos of grieving parents warning students about hazing, demanding changes in the laws, or renewed accountability of institutions both fraternal and academic.

These are pleas that often fall on deaf ears because their focus is mostly on the victimizers, those who promote and encourage this behavior—and the simple truth is . . . victimizers don't care. While the average student will gaze upon these lectures and these videos, and certainly will feel sorry for the grieving party, they will still be of the mindset, "They aren't talking about me, I don't haze and I wouldn't be hazed, I would never do that, I'd quit first."

But they are wrong. Some are too close to the mirror to see their own reflection. The gradual creep of complacency and groupthink is as subtle as a slow-growing cancer, and young people simply don't know what they don't know.

On our part, there has to be a shift in philosophical teaching when it comes to this behavior. We have to realize that what we think we know about the socialization of youth through the centuries has literally been turned upside down by social media, COVID-19, and a whole host of seismic changes in culture and thinking.

We have come to believe that a high school résumé stuffed full of activities that point toward socialization and popularity is the "right stuff" for the manicured path to adulthood. We just might be wrong.

"Great kid, very popular, lots of friends." These words have been uttered at far too many funerals of young people who fall victim to hazing or coercive behavior. But these are also the same words uttered at the same funerals for those who made a conscious decision to stay and not walk away when it was in their best interest to do just that. "Fuck you, I'm not doing that" needs to roll off their tongues as easily as "I love you, Mom; I love you, Dad." How do we get there?

While popularity might point to a happy, well-adjusted kid, capable of making friends, it also might be a sign that your kid NEEDS to have a lot of friends and a constant stream of social interactions. There is a difference with being popular and *needing* to be popular. This need for 24/7 socialization, from social media to social venues, is the crack cocaine of this generation and it just may be the real drug that leads them to chug that shot, or snort that line, or pop that "bar" of Xanax, or permit themselves to be locked in a room with a mandate of "don't you leave until you drink it all." It is their oxygen. We have to show them there are other ways to breathe.

I like to think that COVID-19 and the abrupt cessation of crowd socialization may have helped young people realize that they can survive without the fear of missing out, but I'm not so sure. Our ERs are stuffed to the gills lately of young people in the throes of major depression and suicidality, so many seem sadder and are starving for friendship and social interaction. I fear this may lead to a kind of caution-blindness on their part.

"Hell, when I went to college I picked up and went across the country to get away from all my friends, to start anew, to grow as a person, as an individual," my partner and fellow ER physician Dr. Krug told me. "I'm not so sure these kids are ready for all this." I tend to agree.

We have to teach incoming students that the transition to adulthood is a singular road of individual self-discovery and that, while magical, it is riddled with potholes of those who will pressure, coerce, haze, and lead them to that needle and bottle and wheel and bridge if they are not of solid mind and armed with the shield-of-will to say NO. Should they be without this armor, they have no business being in college.

The fall school year of 2021 was unprecedented, and as an Emergency Physician I saw more deaths from reckless college behavior than we have ever seen before. We are looking at two years' worth of students dumped into one milieu who have had little time to howl at the moon, socialize, and grow on top with being behind academically. There will be a surge in drug- and alcohol-related problems and mental health issues on college campuses. I fear that colleges across the country are ill-prepared for this, so it is up to us, the parents, to arm our students now. Give them the tools, have the hard talks with them, really look at them and ask yourself if they have the inner determination to be their own person no matter how many prom courts they stood in or student governing positions they held, or captains of sports they were awarded. College will always be there, but don't count on colleges to protect them. That's up to you.

So as a seasoned ER doc, I would ask that you start NOW. Hold them in your arms, peer into their eyes, tell them what the world will look like to you if they die, how you won't survive, how you will never be happy again. Make them see the love you have for them. Arm them with the "shield of NO." Listen to them, don't be afraid to bring them home if you sense they aren't ready—this isn't a race against other students. Don't compare your kid to the one down the street—they are all unique, so love them uniquely.

Be diligent and aware this school year, listen with open ears, see with open eyes, and love with a full heart.

"Great kid, very popular, lots of friends." These words should only be uttered at birthdays and weddings.

Never at a funeral.

Dr. Louis M. Profeta is a nationally recognized, award-winning writer, TED Talk speaker, and Emergency Physician at St. Vincent Hospital of Indianapolis, a level 1 trauma center. He has cared for more than 60,000 patients. He is the best-selling author of the critically acclaimed book *The Patient in Room Nine Says He's God*. He is a dynamic and sought-after public speaker and frequent guest on TV and radio. He has gained critical acclaim for his poignant essays and writings for LinkedIn Pulse Magazine on topics such as our national heroin crisis in *When the Lion Kills Your Child*, end-of-life care in *I Know You Love Me, Now Let Me Die*, and dozens of similar essays. In 2015, 2016, and 2017 he was named LinkedIn Top Voice for readership in health care. His scathingly sarcastic but passionate essay *Your Kid and My Kid Aren't Playing in the Pros* was honored as one of the best articles on sports by the Society of Professional

Journalism. In 2018, he was honored by the National Society of Newspaper Columnists for outstanding contribution to online media. His essays entitled *A Sunday Talk on Sex, Drugs, Drinking, and Dying* and *A Very Dangerous Place for a Child Is College* may be the most read and shared essays in history on the topic of drugs, sexual assault, and alcohol abuse on college campuses, having been read by millions. His 2018 essay *I'll Look at Your Facebook Profile Before I Tell Your Mother You're Dead* has become one of the most read articles in the world on social media.

Following the success of *A Sunday Talk on Sex, Drugs, Drinking, and Dying*, Dr. Profeta has been invited to speak all over the country on this topic. Dr. Profeta has told hundreds of parents their children have been killed over his career and he brings this reality to campuses across America. Some have described this as the most brutal, realistic, and impactful presentation ever given on the topic. He is rapidly becoming recognized as one of the most widely read opinion essayists in America today, including LinkedIn Top Voice in Health Care in 2020.

You can see Dr. Profeta's presentations here:
www.greekuniversity.org/louis

Email Dr. Profeta: louermd@att.net

CHAPTER 14

Challenging Cultural Appropriation and Blackface on Campus:
A Beginner's Guide to Anti-Racism

**Shyam K. Sriram, PhD and
Stacy Cavanaugh**

| *Glossary*

Cultural Appropriation: Theft and/or exploitative use of elements of a culture other than your own without understanding of their cultural meaning or significance

Anti-Racist: A person who takes consistent action on a daily basis to dismantle systemic racism and anti-blackness

Anti-Blackness: A pervasive ideology in American culture that black lives and people are devalued compared to white lives

Privilege: Unearned benefits of a given social group which grants them power within society

White Supremacy: The ideology that white people and their ideas, thoughts, and actions are superior to People of Color (POC) and their ideas, thoughts, and actions

Introduction

- In December 2012, the Nu Gamma chapter of Chi Omega at Penn State University held a "Mexican-themed" party. A photo showed about twenty-five, mostly-white women wearing sombreros, fake mustaches, and ponchos, holding signs like "Will Mow Lawn for Weed and Beer." The chapter was closed permanently in 2014.[62]
- The Beta Xi chapter of Tau Kappa Epsilon at Arizona State University hosted a racist, "MLK Party" in January 2014 to coincide with Dr. Martin Luther King Jr. Day. Guests were encouraged to wear sports jerseys, hip hop attire, and mimic Black culture. The chapter was immediately banned and kicked off campus permanently.[63]

---

[62] Kat Stoeffel, "Penn State Sorority's Mexican Fiesta Backfires," *The Cut*, December 5, 2012, https://www.thecut.com/2012/12/penn-state-sororitys-mexican-fiesta-backfires.html.

[63] Anne Ryman, "Fraternity expelled over MLK-themed party," *USA Today*, January 23, 2014, https://www.usatoday.com/story/news/

Both of these incidents highlight the disturbing trend of fraternities and sororities engaging in racist practices and cultural appropriation under the guise of "social events" and "having a good time." Every year, Greeks are criticized for participating in events that are often viewed as ignorant, sexist, culturally inappropriate, or disrespectful, and every year, most of the perpetrators claim they did not know it was wrong—or worse, ask, "Why is everyone so sensitive?" This chapter introduces the concept of cultural appropriation and challenges students to think about how they can truly engage in anti-racist work by holding their peers on campus accountable for social events that might appropriate or disrespect the cultural traditions of others.

What Is Cultural Appropriation?

The term *cultural appropriation* refers to the taking of traditional knowledge, cultural expressions, rituals, aesthetic standards, or artifacts of a different culture without permission. Cultural appropriation can feel ambiguous, and its nuances are often either unknown or ignored. Typically, cultural appropriation occurs when a member of a dominant culture adopts aspects of culture from an oppressed or marginalized group.

There are several reasons that cultural appropriation is problematic. It can involve the perpetuation of stereotypes, as the practice of blackface did in the nineteenth and early twentieth centuries. Costumes for Halloween or ethnically-

nation/2014/01/23/fraternity-expelled-over-mlk-themed-party/4811083/.

themed parties are often worn to get a laugh, a clear indicator that you are perpetuating a stereotype.

These acts of appropriation often occur without any knowledge or understanding of the cultural meaning or significance of the objects or practices being taken. Culturally appropriated objects and practices are often then commodified and sold by major corporations, essentially erasing their cultural meaning and significance.

Common pushback against accusations of cultural appropriation often includes cries of "What's the big deal?" and "Don't they have better things to worry about?" We would like you to know that it *is* a big deal. That is because cultural appropriation treats all aspects of oppressed cultures as free for the taking while disregarding the origins and significance of what is being taken. This taking of culture promotes the erasure and invisibility of the culture from which the artifact originated.

CULTURAL APPROPRIATION FLOW CHART

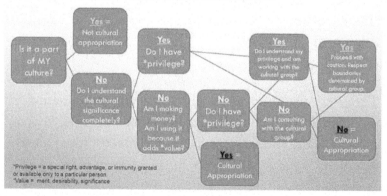

There are some simple things that you can ask yourself to avoid cultural appropriation.[64] First, is the item in question part of your culture? A white woman wearing a Native headdress to a music festival would be engaging in cultural appropriation because she is wearing an item of significance to a specific culture that she does not belong to. Next you can ask yourself if you understand the cultural significance of the item or practice. Native American cultures traditionally use white sage and other herbal medicines in ceremonies that are deeply rooted in spiritual meaning. But the health and wellness industry has co-opted the Native American practice of smudging or smoke cleansing. Today, the sacred practice of smudging has been so commodified that you can buy white sage at Urban Outfitters.

Another major indicator of whether or not you are engaging in cultural appropriation involves some self-reflection. Ask yourself whether you hold more privilege than the group whose cultural practices you are adopting. You have racial privilege if your life wasn't made more difficult because of your skin color. If you do have privilege and are adopting elements of another culture, then you are likely appropriating. This ties in with the next indicator that you are engaging in cultural appropriation—financial benefit from items of a culture that is not your own. This type of cultural appropriation frequently occurs when a style of cultural art is mass produced and sold by a corporation. This is both cultural appropriation and the commodification of culture.

---

[64] https://www.reddit.com/r/IndianCountry/comments/cctir2/cultural_appropriation_flow_chart/

What Is Not Cultural Appropriation?

There is a difference between cultural appreciation and cultural appropriation. Engaging with a culture and its people with genuine respect, interest, and desire to learn is not considered cultural appropriation. A person of another culture who is invited to a traditional Indian wedding may wear traditional Indian attire (saree) as a sign of respect for the culture, just as a Jewish woman visiting a mosque (Muslim house of worship) might cover her hair with a scarf. Studying traditional music and dance from any culture or country is also not cultural appropriation because you are learning about the roots and history and have been given permission to learn and then teach others by the founders of those art forms. These are not acts of cultural appropriation. The difference lies in the engagement with the culture and not just the adoption and perpetuation of stereotypes.

In matters of purchasing cultural art and artifacts, cultural appropriation depends upon whom you purchased it from. If you respect and admire Native Indigenous art and purchase a piece of jewelry from an Indigenous craftsperson to occasionally wear, that is not cultural appropriation. However, if you purchase a mass produced "Navajo" blanket from Target and have no connection to that culture, you are engaging in cultural appropriation.

Why Does It Matter to College Life?

As you navigate college life, you may be exposed to instances of cultural appropriation, or question whether you yourself are participating in cultural appropriation. You may be invited to a Cinco de Mayo party where costumes are encouraged, or you may consider wearing a Halloween costume of a person of a different race. Your best friend may apply her makeup in such a way that her complexion resembles that of a woman of color when your friend is not (also known as blackfishing). You may be asked to sexualize a costume or ethnic dress that is not normally seen as sexual.

Before you put on a potentially offensive costume for the sake of fun, think about your motivations for wanting to do so. If you are trying to get a laugh, you are likely perpetuating offensive stereotypes. If your costume is an attempt to represent or mock a culture that you don't belong to, you are also likely engaging in cultural appropriation.

Blackface, which was once a form of entertainment across the United States, gave white people the power to imitate Black people and Black bodies for the sake of laughs. Minstrel shows were performed across the United States, even for President Lincoln in the White House, and for many Americans, minstrelsy became the primary vehicle of information about Black people. Most people know that blackface is racist, demeaning, vulgar, and absolutely unacceptable. Yet every year, Americans, including college students, wear blackface during Halloween. Why? How come it never ends? Some scholars say it is about a history of racism in America and a legacy of white supremacy that always elevates white culture and white people above others while simultaneously depressing people of color and their heritages. Others argue that it is simply about a lack of accountability.

What Does It Mean to Be Anti-Racist?

There are no hard and fast rules on how to be an anti-racist. The process of becoming an anti-racist involves two main strategies: inner work and outward action. Much of the personal work around anti-racism involved unlearning the lies of white supremacy and learning about the ways in which POC have been historically marginalized and oppressed in the United States. You will also need to recognize the ways in which you have benefitted from and participated in this marginalization and oppression. Being an anti-racist involves conceding some of your privileges to help others attain equity.

Anti-racism is about taking actions, however big or small, to dismantle white supremacy and systemic racism. Being an anti-racist is not about the performative allyship of a black square on Instagram. While being an ally is a good start, what the anti-racism movement needs are accomplices and disruptors. To quote the great John Lewis, the movement needs people who are prepared to get into "good trouble."[65]

This is by no means an exhaustive list, but here are some ways that you can engage in anti-racist action:

- Have brave conversations with friends and relatives about race and racism.
- If you see something say something, regardless of social mores or your level of discomfort. If

---

[65] Joshua Bote, "'Get in good trouble, necessary trouble': Rep. John Lewis in his own words," *USA Today*, July 18, 2020, https://www.usatoday.com/story/news/politics/2020/07/18/rep-john-lewis-most-memorable-quotes-get-good-trouble/5464148002/.

you hear a racist comment or witness an act of discrimination, speak up about it in the moment.

- Listen to and uplift the voices of POC on campus and in your personal life.
- Speak out in opposition to themed parties that encourage and celebrate cultural appropriation.
- Identify and fight against racist policies and practices.
- Learn about the racial wealth gap and the fight for reparations.
- Contact your legislators in support of racial justice legislation.
- Speak out/call in when someone is wearing an offensive and culturally appropriative Halloween costume.

Finally, and perhaps most importantly, understand that being anti-racist is something you will never arrive at; you will never finish your anti-racist work. You must approach your anti-racism from a place of humility and acknowledge that you will never be done learning. Anti-racism is not about perfection; it is about taking actionable steps to dismantle systemic racism.

Conclusion

We believe that this information should be widely available to all college students so they understand the very real consequences of engaging in cultural appropriation. You are going to make mistakes on your anti-racism journey, and that is okay. But it is not okay to continue to engage in an offensive practice once you know your behavior is problematic. Our goal is to arm students with the knowledge to make the best decisions for themselves, their peers, and their chapters in order to strengthen communities and truly build unity. Activism without intention and education is just performative.

We also recognize how difficult it can be to hold your brothers and sisters in Greek organizations accountable for their actions. We encourage you to be brave and remember what Dr. Cornel West said: "Never forget that justice is what love looks like in public."[66]

Case Study

Harun is the social chair for his fraternity and is one of only a handful of brothers of color. He is a hardworking student from an immigrant family and always wanted to get involved in the Greek system because he saw it as a great way to make friends and be part of a brotherhood. During a recent chapter meeting, he asks for suggestions about party themes and someone yells, "COVID!" The room bursts into laughter, but Harun is shocked about the callousness of the idea and then stunned when others chime in about how it might be fun to "dress Asian" and see sorority women as geishas. Harun forces a smile and says that he will think about it.

Two days later, the chapter president asks him what is happening about "the Asian party" because he wants to ask

---

[66] "Cornel West: Justice Is What Love Looks Like in Public," YouTube, April 17, 2011, https://www.youtube.com/watch?v=nGqP7S_WO6o.

out someone in a sorority and Harun says, "Wait, are you serious? I thought we were just joking." The president says that a lot of the guys are really interested and think it might be fun. When Harun mentions that the idea is offensive and demeaning, the president laughs and tells him, "Don't be so serious, man. We are just having a good time. Let me know when you finalize it so I can tell everyone. It's going to be a blast."

Which one of the following solutions is the most appropriate in this scenario?

1. He should immediately contact the faculty advisor or alumni board to get some ideas about what to do.
2. Harun should voice his concerns with the rest of the executive team (e-board) during the next meeting and strenuously oppose the party idea.
3. The rest of the house seems really into an Asian-themed party, so Harun should stop worrying and just enjoy himself.
4. Harun should collaborate with the campus-based diversity office or Department of Asian American Studies to have someone give a talk during chapter on Asian stereotypes.

The best solution here is #4. First, let us discuss what does not work. Just because the majority of brothers want something does not validate its acceptance, so #3 is out. Similarly, although reaching out to the advisor or alumni board seems like a good idea, the reality is that these organizations have little influence on the day-to-day operations of a chapter.

Worse, the alumni board may just be there as representatives of the national organization and may have no incentive to stop the chapter from engaging in any social activity (however racist or problematic) because national organizations can also engage in white privilege and not even realize it.

As a fraternity brother of color in a predominately white chapter and college, Harun has the burden and responsibility of assuming the racial trauma of his fraternity brothers who do not understand the racial history of exclusion in America. While it is important for him to let the rest of the e-board know how he feels (#2), a better solution would be working with his e-board to educate them and then share the educational resources with the rest of the chapter (#4).

Dr. Shyam Sriram has been involved in the fields of secondary and higher education since 2003. Since that time he has worked in a variety of capacities which have allowed him to gain experiential knowledge at every level of the educational industry (high school to community college to PhD-granting institutions). He taught at Morehouse College, Georgia State University, the University of California at Santa Barbara, Georgia Perimeter College, Butler University, and the College of Charleston. Additionally, he spent a year working at two private, Islamic schools in suburban Chicago; two summers mentoring inner-city high school students in Atlanta; and several summers grading Advanced Placement exams. He has taught, collaborated with, and mentored thousands of students; and realizes now, more than ever, the need for quality professionals in higher education who are not just great teachers, but great administrators as well. He recently joined the faculty of Gonzaga University as a lecturer in the Department of Political Science.

He received his BA in Political Science in 2002 from Purdue University where he was a member of the Alpha Phi chapter of Alpha Chi Rho Fraternity. He also has an MA in Political Science from Georgia State University and a second MA and PhD in Political Science from the University of California at Santa Barbara.

You can see Dr. Sriram's presentations here:
www.greekuniversity.org/shyam

Email Dr. Sriram: shyam@greekuniversity.org

Stacy Cavanaugh is a white, cisgender, bisexual woman living in Denver, Colorado. She is a mother, an anti-racist, a leftist, and a feminist. Born and raised in Flint, Michigan, she realized early the impacts and intersections of race, class, and gender on individuals and society. She holds a Bachelor of Arts in Sociology from the University of Michigan - Flint and a Master's of Social Work from Metropolitan State University of Denver. Her research interests include police violence and qualified immunity, adverse childhood experiences, residential displacement, and reparations for Black Americans. Stacy is fascinated with social theory and imagines a world where people can thrive beyond the oppressive forces of racism and capitalism. She spends her free time performing comedic improv and riding her bicycle in Denver.

Email Stacy: cavanaughstacy@gmail.com

CHAPTER 15

Tools for Change:
Introduction of a New Model for Member Initiation

Dr. Kim Bullington

> Think of ritual as if our founders were speaking to us across time. . . . Ritual is like a modern-day picture in an antique frame. . . . The ideas, the principles, the hopes, the dreams, the faith that the rituals expressed are too big for words. You need more than just words to pass these on. You've got to have ceremony. You've got to have all the richness, all the different aspects as we know them.
>
> —Greg Hauser[67]

All of us are taught to live by our Ritual. It is the one thing that unites us as sisters and brothers. It is the one common thread that we all share. It is

---

[67] Greg Hauser, Former President of the North American Interfraternity Conference, "Sharing Our Ritual" video (1994).

what guides us to become better people. Edward M. King, a member of Sigma Chi, in his essay, "The Secret Thoughts of the Ritual," took a powerful stance and wrote as if a Ritual was a person. In it, he likens Ritual to a road map and asks and answers three poignant questions:

1. Who am I? Your ritual.
2. What am I? A system of values.
3. What am I for? My purpose is not to make you just a better fraternity man [or woman], but more importantly, a better human being.[68]

Think to how your Ritual guides you. What aspects are important to you? I know my Ritual intimately. I have helped initiate thousands of women into my organization. Every time I see my sisters in a Ritual activity, I find another thing that I love about it—what do you love about yours? How do you incorporate the values from your Ritual into your daily life; and if you don't do this, why not?

Ritual does not begin at the first pinning . . . nor does it end at initiation or even graduation. Ritual should be a part of the collegiate experience, and beyond. Living the ideals of your Ritual can help instill characteristics of brotherhood and sisterhood; living your Ritual can provide structure, increase fraternal bonds, and decrease negative actions such as hazing. Think about your Ritual—I can guarantee that nowhere in there does it say that you should treat another member poorly or make them go through something that

---

[68] Edward M. King, "The Secret Thoughts of a Ritual," https://www.fandm. edu/uploads/files/720054002341408493-secret-thoughts-of-a-ritual-original.pdf.

makes them uncomfortable, unwanted, or different/*othered*. And I can guarantee that your Ritual guides you to love and support each other.

The past few years have been a call to action for Greek Letter Organizations (GLOs). The COVID-19 pandemic certainly played a role in creating change, but so did the pivot in society to move to a more inclusive and equitable society. But before we talk about the present, or even the future, we must take a trip to the 1700s to 1900s because they provide context to this . . . *chapter* (yes, insert lame Greek-Life dad joke here).

A Slow Beginning

In 1776, five students established Phi Beta Kappa at the College of William & Mary. It was created as a literary society of *"unalienable Brothers"* from the Masonic tradition,[69] and had a nomination and initiation process.[70] It also met the intellectual and social needs that the classrooms were not providing. The growth of Phi Beta Kappa was slow, but in the 1880s, Phi Beta Kappa transformed and reemerged as an organized brotherhood that had a "motto, a medal or badge, a grip, a seal, a constitution, a form of initiation, regular meetings, literary exercises, social occasions, the name 'Fraternity', the bond of brotherhood and the idea of

---

[69] Oscar M. Voorhees, "The Phi Beta Kappa at William and Mary," *The Phi Beta Kappa Key*, Vol. 1 No. 7 (March 1912), https://www.jstor.org/stable/pdf/42913634.pdf.

[70] G. Kurt Piehler, "Phi Beta Kappa: The Invention of an Academic Tradition," *History of Education Quarterly*, Vol. 28, No. 2 (Summer 1988), 207–29, https://www.jstor.org/stable/368490.

expansion."[71] Although Phi Beta Kappa later evolved into a prestigious honor society, it is one of the first organized secret societies and, more importantly, it is the precursor to the fraternities and sororities[72] that we know today.

Expansion, Expansion, Expansion

As early as 1825, the Kappa Alpha Society was established at Union College and used many of Phi Beta Kappa's practices. Soon after, Sigma Phi and Delta Phi were established. These three groups were established based on the concept of brotherhood and referred to themselves as fraternities. As they expanded onto other campuses, other organizations quickly followed. At Wesleyan College, the Adelphean Society was formed in 1851, followed by the Philomathean Society the next year—these organizations eventually became Alpha Delta Pi and Phi Mu. Kappa Alpha Theta was formed as a Greek society at DePauw University. These societies for women were soon generally referred to as sororities in the same tradition as the male fraternities. Not long after, other organizations, based on race and/or religion quickly followed and by the 1920s, there were over 100 fraternities and 38 sororities at local and national levels.

Fraternities and sororities of old were based on homogeneity, exclusion, and were largely stratified. It was not until the 1960s that fraternities and sororities removed race-based

---

[71] Voorhees, "The Phi Beta Kappa at William and Mary," 11.

[72] While I use the term *sorority*, generally, it is important to acknowledge there are women's fraternities. Over half of the National Pan-Hellenic Conference organizations are women's fraternities (National Pan-Hellenic Conference, 2021).

exclusions.[73] The expansion of GLOs continues today, and while some are the organizations founded in the late 1800s and early 1900s, there are Greek social organizations that continue to be created based on the needs of its membership and to maintain stability of the organization.

The Development of the Ritual

One of the things all of us who are initiated into a Greek Letter Organization share is our Ritual. This Ritual, for the most part, was conceived in the very early beginnings of our respective organizations. This means that most of them were written in the mid-1800s to the mid-1900s. While we embrace and value our Ritual, we do need to realize a few things.

Three Things are Inevitable: Death, Taxes . . . and Language Change

Back when most of our Rituals were written, the language was, frankly, different. While we still understand the meaning of (most of) the words, there are many archaic phrases that have changed over the years; gone are words like *devoirs* (responsibilities), *tapers* (small candles), and the use of *thou* and *thee*. And it's not only the words that have changed, but many of the phrases that were common back then no longer are today. For example, we no longer ask others *"How came you so . . .?"* ("How did you come to be . . .?") nor do we

---

[73] Matthew W. Hughey, "A paradox of participation: Nonwhites in White sororities and fraternities," (2010) *Social Problems* 57 (4): 653–79.

accuse someone of being a *hugger-mugger* (underhanded). There was also an expectation that members were familiar with foreign languages like Greek, Latin, and French, and some of these words most likely appear in initiation rituals for many organizations. In fact, I often find myself smiling as I see current new members trying to navigate and pronounce these now-awkward stylistic machinations and remember my own time struggling with them as well.

Religion

Many of our rituals are based on the Bible. Let's think back to the beginnings of American higher education—many of the institutions created in the first hundred years of the United States of America had strong ties to a religious Christian denomination.[74] Many of the GLOs founded during these times were founded on Judeo-Christian values like love, loyalty, faithfulness, honesty. Considering the times, and the role religion played in American society, it is not surprising that ritual and religion are connected.

Exclusion

Fraternities and sororities are exclusive societies. In the past, many of our recruitment strategies were based on exclusion versus inclusion. Some recruited for looks, athletic ability, money, but the lucky ones recruited for fit and potential to grow the organization. Although the following quote is

---

[74] John R. Thelin, *A History of American Higher Education* 3rd ed. (Baltimore: John Hopkins University Press, 2019).

based on sorority exclusivity, it fits for both fraternities and sororities:

> Membership in sororities was based, not only on personal congeniality, but on the individual's ability to share expenses as well. Students outside sororities contributed to perpetuating them by too often believing that they were being left out of something valuable.[75]

As fraternities and sororities have, for the most part, moved from more exclusionary practices, it's time to take a look into how to become more inclusive and equitable and embrace the diversification of fraternities and sororities.

Reimagining Our Ritual

This chapter is not designed to force your organizations to change your ritual; it does, however, serve as a call to consider your rituals in the light of language change, religion, and exclusion. It is not meant to change the meaning behind the ritual, but as society moves to a more diverse, equitable, and inclusive (DEI) environment, it may be time to fraternities and sororities to examine their rituals in a DEI lens.

Inter/National DEI Committee

Forming a DEI committee or taskforce on the inter/ national level is one of the first steps an organization should

---

[75] Barbara Miller Solomon, *In the Company of Educated Women* (New Haven, CT: Yale University Press, 1985), 107.

consider. The makeup of the committee should be one that is representative of the membership as a whole, but also representative of the organization's minority populations. These members should be aware of minority members' needs and desires. Also, it is important to look through DEI through several different lenses and uncover diversity across and within the organization's groups. A successful DEI effort will examine diversity, equity, and inclusion based on several factors including race, but also through disability (i.e., physical, mental limitations), cognition and neurodivergency (how the brain deals with learning and other mental conditions), religious or lack thereof, and even possibly trauma-informed conditions (e.g., removing one of the senses). These areas should be examined within the organization's policies, rituals, and practices.

Be Prepared

Change is not always easy, especially when change can affect deeply-seated traditions. It is important to be aware, and to acknowledge, that members will be on varying sides of the spectrum—from those who vehemently oppose any change to a Ritual because of tradition and to honor the founders, to those who completely embrace the change to better the experience for all members. And although change can be necessary, it is important to hear all the voices and to encourage conversations and move them forward into spaces that are open, respectful, and understanding of differences of opinion.

What Needs Changing? . . .

. . . And more importantly—what doesn't need to change? This answer will vary greatly by organization, but thinking in the lenses of diversity, equity, and inclusion, what changes can be made to make the organization more welcoming to its members and to its potential members? What can change? What absolutely cannot? Who will be affected, and to what extent will they be affected? Will the organization lose membership, or will this change allow the organization to grow even more? There are myriad decisions that must be considered when making changes to any organization, but these are particularly important issues to consider.

Communication

Once DEI recommendations are received, organizations should hold focus groups and townhalls—both in person and online—to hear from current collegiate as well as alumni on the process of becoming more diverse, inclusive, and equitable. These meetings should not only provide information on why the organization is considering a change, but also emphasize that the change will be based on top-down/bottom-up decisions based upon the feedback from the membership. If nothing else, the communication that goes out should focus on making members' experiences more meaningful while continuing to recognize the foundations on which the organization was founded.

It is important to recognize that all organizations have different mechanisms in place to enact change. Organization leadership should clearly communicate the process of any change, especially one that is so integral to the foundation of the organization like Ritual. Timelines, minutes, and decision processes should be made transparent to the membership.

Now What?

While a change to Ritual may not be palatable to some, it is important to consider that one of the scariest things is not changing with the times. With the negative focus on Greek organizations and moves to abolish Greek Life, it is more important than ever that we look at our practices to ensure that we are providing opportunities for growth for all of our members; we need to embrace the diversity that makes our groups stronger, and we need to remove barriers that separate us. We should examine our rituals through the values that they engender, and not always the words in which they were written. Words have power, whether that power is positive or negative is up to the interpretation of the end user. While this chapter is by no means a call to change Ritual so drastically that it changes what the Rituals were based upon, it is a call to examine our practices, including Ritual, through a lens that is diverse, equitable, and inclusive for all of our members. Change is not easy, but reluctance to change for the wrong reasons is downright terrifying.

A Case Study

Jenna was thrilled when she received her bid to join the top sorority on campus. She had a wonderful new member experience, and she knew that she was about to be initiated into a group that encouraged her and challenged her to become a better person. A few days before initiation, Jenna attended a mandatory pre-initiation meeting. At the meeting, there were several things discussed to prepare the new members for the upcoming initiation. They went over the organization and chapter bylaws. They discussed the beginnings of the organization and how it was founded based on Christian beliefs and ideals. As a proud Atheist, Jenna was slightly taken aback. The members with whom she had been interacting never discussed religion and what part it played within the sorority. Jenna spoke with her new member class and brought up her concerns. No one else seemed to be bothered by the religious aspect of the impending initiation ceremony but her. So, she decided to go through with it, after all she loved the chapter members and got along with all of them, plus she'd already paid her initiation and badge fees.

When it was time for Jenna to be initiated, she was brought into the Ritual room. During the Ritual, there were numerous references to the Bible and to God, which made Jenna uncomfortable and feel that her Atheism was not even being considered, and she began to notice things that made her uncomfortable, such as how the members were standing, how the room was decorated, the words of the Ritual that she was hearing. Nevertheless, she went on with the ceremony and became a fully initiated member, despite her misgivings.

Three weeks after initiation, Jenna terminated her membership because she knew she would never be able to reconcile her Atheism and the Christian beliefs on which the organization was founded.

Questions to Consider

1. What could have been done differently?
    a. Jenna
    b. Chapter
    c. Inter/national organization?

2. How could the chapter and inter/national organization have better prepared Jenna and the other new members earlier in the new member process rather than a few days prior to initiation?

3. What would you have done if you were:
    a. Jenna
    b. Chapter officer
    c. Inter/national organization leader

4. Take a look at your organization. Are they following a path to diversity, equity, and inclusion? What have they done to make members' experiences better in this area? What have they not done?

5. What would you do?

Dr. Bullington's career at Old Dominion University spans both academic and student affairs. Her experience in Admissions coupled with her administrative work in the Department of Engineering Management and Systems Engineering make her uniquely placed to understand both areas of higher education. She works actively to bridge the silos and bring people together and remove barriers to education and communication.

Dr. Bullington continues to seek to expand her knowledge through her research on at-risk student populations. Dr. Bullington serves as the Co-editor-in-Chief for the Higher Education Politics and Economics journal and is an adjunct professor in the Educational Foundations and Leadership program at Old Dominion University.

Email Kim: kbulling@odu.edu

Call to Action

Michael Ayalon

W hat an amazing opportunity we have in front of us! Fraternities and sororities have exactly what Gen Z is looking for in terms of networking, jobs, careers, and mentors. Both of my parents were from another country, so I did not know about fraternities at all when I attended the University at Buffalo as an undergraduate. There are so many first-generation students on your campus today who don't know anything about fraternities or sororities, and there are also students on our campus who don't really care about the fraternity/sorority experience. However, there are three questions that all students ask themselves when they arrive on campus, and will continue to ask at various points of their college career:

1. "Will I make friends here?"
2. "Will I be excluded somehow?"
3. "Do I even belong in college?"

Fraternities and sororities have the unique ability to help ease these concerns that every student has. When we look at Maslow's Hierarchy of Needs, we see where fraternities and sororities excel: belongingness and love. If not for the fraternity/sorority, I would have never been able to figure out how to interact with the 30,000 students at my institution, and I might not be a college graduate today. We can find that shared purpose in Fraternity and Sorority Life that will help students stay anchored at their institution and retain these students through graduation.

There is one guarantee. College students will experience adversity, especially today as we deal with the fallout of the pandemic. This could include challenging academic courses, financial stress, mental or physical health issues, and even challenging family situations such as a sickness or even death of a loved one. The student's interaction with their fraternity/sorority will help their resiliency in overcoming these issues. Not only are the members themselves supportive, but they also can refer students to campus resources when needed.

It all starts with a feeling of belonging, the critical component that often means the difference between success and failure at college. The new member education process should be facilitating a sense of belonging to our fraternities and sororities, as well as to the larger college campus community. That education process can also continue to feed our sense of belonging as long as it continues through graduation and evolves to reflect the changing needs of the students as they move toward a degree and entering their career.

That brings me to an important concept mentioned in the introduction of this book. How can we structure our new member education process to focus more on "love and belonging" from Maslow's Hierarchy of Needs into our fraternities and sororities, and reduce some of the current focus on "rites of passage" that can lead to hazing? When we look at sexual assault cases or hazing cases, the commonality is a big power differential between the abuser and the victim. When you see sexual assaults happening, many times the abuser is a boss, coach, or teacher, and they are using their power over others to reach their victims.

One way to reduce the power differentials between non-initiated members and initiated members in fraternities and sororities is to assume that all undergraduate members are on a journey toward college graduation. After all, isn't that the goal? If we have an undergraduate who ignores academics but puts all of his/her time into the organization, while they might have reached initiation in the fraternity/sorority, they ultimately can't contribute to the organization because they might have flunked out of school. How does that help our organizations? Unfortunately, I continually see this happening.

Perhaps it is time to make *graduation the goal* and align the goals of fraternity/sorority with the goals of our host institutions to create a better partnership with higher education and really promote academics/scholarship as a way of differentiating our experience from non-affiliated students. It becomes a higher bar for students to strive for on college campuses.

To become an Eagle Scout, one must be involved in their troop for at least six months as a Life Scout, show dedication to Scout Oath and Scout Law over time, provide references from family, work, church, and other community groups, earn twenty-one merit badges, serve at least six months in a leadership position, carry out an Eagle service project, attend a Scoutmaster conference, and pass a board of review. If we compare that to the fraternity/sorority experience, typically new members in a fraternity/sorority only have an eight-week new member program!

What if there were twenty-one "merit badges" in a variety of areas within fraternity/sorority life, and these focus areas would develop over an educational program that took place over *all four years* to keep our members engaged throughout their undergraduate experience? While we might not eliminate all hazing incidents, the power differential would be lessened between all new members who are actually on a four-year journey to reach initiation at graduation. Here are other positives:

- It would help our retention rates.
- It would help to create more engaged alumni for our organizations because they have been active participants all four years.
- Apathy in our fraternity/sorority would be reduced.
- Fraternity/sorority would be more relevant as students' needs change over their four-year college experience.
- We would reduce the number of hazing incidents that occur in our organizations.

- We would be aligned perfectly with our host institutions and their goal of student success dynamics which include retention, graduation rates, and job/graduate school placement rates.

By changing the endgame for incoming freshmen from earning their letters in a relatively short amount of time to persevering and earning their membership throughout their four-year college experience, perhaps the bar would be raised in all fraternities and sororities to create more productive and dynamic members.

I hope this book has motivated you to reevaluate your new member education process and ask whether or not we are meeting the needs of today's students. Should you need any assistance on your campus, in your council, or in your chapter, please reach out so we can help.

Wishing you all the best in your lifelong member education journey.

Michael Ayalon

www.greekuniversity.org

"An organization's ability to learn, and translate that learning into action rapidly is the ultimate competitive advantage."

—*Jack Welch*